£2.50

Penguin Education
Penguin Library of Physical Sciences

Waves
J. P.

R. P. Williams

Waves

J. P. G. Richards and R. P. Williams

Penguin Books

Penguin Books Ltd, Harmondsworth, Middlesex, England
Penguin Books Inc, 7110 Ambassador Road, Baltimore, Md 21207, USA
Penguin Books Australia Ltd, Ringwood, Victoria, Australia

First published 1972
Copyright © J. P. G. Richards and R. P. Williams, 1972

Made and printed in Great Britain by
William Clowes & Sons Limited
London, Colchester and Beccles
Set in Monotype Times

Contents

Editorial Foreword 7

1 **Introduction** 9

1.1 What are waves? 9
1.2 Description of some waves we shall study 10

2 **The Theory of Vibrations** 15

2.1 The importance of vibration theory in the understanding of waves 15
2.2 Vibrations of a single particle 15
2.3 Vibrations of two coupled particles: Normal modes 23
2.4 Systems with more than two particles 32

3 **Mathematical Description of Wave Motion** 34

3.1 Waves in one dimension: The function $y = f(x - ct)$ 34
3.2 Harmonic waves 37
3.3 Exponential representation of a harmonic wave 40
3.4 Waves in two and three dimensions: Wavefronts 42
3.5 Circular and spherical wavefronts 48

4 **Waves in Physical Media** 49

4.1 Introduction 49
4.2 Transverse waves in an infinitely long, stretched elastic string 49
4.3 Longitudinal waves in a fluid (liquid or gas) 51
4.4 Pressure waves in a gas 53
4.5 Longitudinal waves in a rod 55
4.6 Current and voltage waves in a transmission line 56

5   **Further Physical Considerations** 60

5.1   Introduction 60
5.2   Initial and boundary conditions 61
5.3   Partial reflection 72
5.4   Energy in a travelling wave 75

6   **Fourier's Theorem** 79

6.1   Introduction and mathematical discussion 79
6.2   The physical significance of Fourier's theorem 89
6.3   The Fourier transform 91
6.4   The delta function 99

7   **Some Wave Phenomena** 107
7.1   The Doppler effect 107
7.2   Dispersion and group velocity 109
7.3   Modulation 114

8   **Sound** 121

8.1   Introduction 121
8.2   Sound waves in a pipe 122
8.3   Waves on strings 129
8.4   Formants 137
8.5   The perception of sound 140

9   **Light** 145

9.1   The electromagnetic theory of light 145
9.2   Polarization 152
9.3   Interference and diffraction 152
9.4   An instance of light not behaving as a wave 170

10   **Wave Mechanics** 173

10.1   The Schrödinger equation 173
10.2   Physical interpretation of the Schrödinger equation 175
10.3   The Heisenberg uncertainty principle 180

        Further Reading 183

        Problems 185

        Acknowledgements 189

        Index 190

Editorial Foreword

For many years, now, the teaching of physics at the first-degree level has posed a problem of organization and selection of material of ever-increasing difficulty. From the teacher's point of view, to pay scant attention to the groundwork is patently to court disaster; from the student's, to be denied the excitement of a journey to the frontiers of knowledge is to be denied his birthright. The remedy is not easy to come by. Certainly, the physics section of the Penguin Library of Physical Sciences does not claim to provide any ready-made solution of the problem. What it is designed to do, instead, is to bring together a collection of compact texts, written by teachers of wide experience, around which undergraduate courses of a 'modern', even of an adventurous, character may be built.

The texts are organized generally at three levels of treatment, corresponding to the three years of an honours curriculum, but there is nothing sacrosanct in this classification. Very probably, most teachers will regard all the first-year topics as obligatory in any course, but, in respect of the others, many patterns of interweaving may commend themselves, and prove equally valid in practice. The list of projected third-year titles is necessarily the longest of the three, and the invitation to discriminating choice is wider, but even here care has been taken to avoid, as far as possible, the post-graduate monograph. The series as a whole (some five first-year, six second-year and fourteen third-year titles) is directed primarily to the undergraduate; it is designed to help the teacher to resist the temptation to overload his course, either with the outmoded legacies of the nineteenth century, or with the more speculative digressions of the twentieth. It is expository, only: it does not attempt to provide either student or teacher with exercises for his tutorial classes, or with mass-produced questions for examinations. Important as this provision may be, responsibility for it must surely lie ultimately with the teacher: he alone knows the precise needs of his students – as they change from year to year.

Within the broad framework of the series, individual authors have rightly regarded themselves as free to adopt a personal approach to the choice and presentation of subject matter. To impose a rigid conformity on a writer is to dull the impact of the written word. This general licence has been extended even to the matter of units. There is much to be said, in theory, in favour of a single system of units of measurement – and it has not been overlooked that national policy in advanced countries is moving rapidly towards uniformity under the

Système International (SI units) – but fluency in the use of many systems is not to be despised: indeed, its acquisition may further, rather than retard, the physicist's education.

A general editor's foreword, almost by definition, is first written when the series for which he is responsible is more nearly complete in his imagination (or the publisher's) than as a row of books on his bookshelf. As these words are penned, that is the nature of the relevant situation: hope has inspired the present tense, in what has just been written, when the future would have been the more realistic. Optimism is one attitude that a general editor must never disown!

N. F.

Chapter 1
Introduction

1 What are waves?

A wave is a curiously difficult entity to define, but the title of this work indicates that the authors should attempt a definition – or at least discuss why a definition should be so difficult. Let us start by trying to imagine how the 'man-in-the-street' would answer the question 'What is a wave?'. He would surely be unable to give a coherent answer, but at least two different significant ingredients might emerge. He might talk about waves on the surface of water and would describe them as 'moving along'. On the other hand, he might refer to the waves in a person's hair which, although they do not appear to move, indicate one property of waves which is to do with shape. So we arrive at the idea of a particular undulating shape moving along. If we now force him to concentrate on this aspect, and ask him to give us some examples of waves, he might well produce the idea that if he shakes one end of a piece of string or cord (say a clothes line) then the movement (or disturbance) travels along the length of the cord; this he would describe as a wave. Furthermore, he might assert that both sound and light are waves. When invited to expound upon any conceivable connection between sound and light, on the one hand, and waves on a clothes line, on the other, he might well become rather unsure, but, if he were the assertive kind, he would probably stick to his guns nevertheless.

And he would be right to do so, for he was correct all along. He had described most of the ingredients of waves without having had a scientific education. Let us try to translate his words into scientific terms.

Waves appear to be disturbances in some sort of medium. In the case of the clothes line the 'medium' was the cord itself and the 'disturbance' was a displacement of part of the cord. The disturbance was carried along by forces which different parts of the cord exerted upon their neighbours. In a similar way, the surface of a pool of water is capable of carrying a disturbance along. Here the 'medium' is the water and the 'disturbance' is an upward (or downward) movement of the surface. Sound waves in air fit into much the same mould. The 'medium' is the air itself and the 'disturbance' is a displacement of a region of the air which, due to the elastic properties of the latter, travels along through the medium.

We have thus gone a long way towards establishing the essential nature of a wave. It is a disturbance of some sort (which may not necessarily be mechanical, as we shall see later) in a medium which, because of the properties of the latter, changes either in form or position, or both, as time goes on.

Let us consider the 'medium' a little further. Although it enables a disturbance to be propagated, it itself does not move bodily along. For example the disturbance at one end of the clothes line is propagated along its length, but none of the particles of which the cord is composed actually moves from one end of the line to the other. So a wave is a means of transmitting energy from one point to another without any net transfer of matter. Moreover, it is a means of transmitting *information* from one point to another. For example, not only does the energy in a sound wave reach our ears and activate our auditory systems, but the manner in which the energy fluctuates with time is capable of interpretation by our brains, enabling us to *perceive* the originally remote signal and (for suitable signals) to make sense of it.

It may have been noticed, during the discussion on the disturbance and the medium, that nothing at all was said about light waves and other forms of radiation such as γ-rays, X-rays, ultraviolet rays, infrared rays and radio waves. The fact is that, while these waves fit generally into the picture we have drawn, they fail to do so in one important respect – they appear to require no medium whatsoever for their propagation. Indeed, although they can travel through some material media (light waves can travel through glass for example) they are not able to do so with as great a speed as they can through a vacuum. This was a source of such great mystery to the nineteenth-century physicist, since it was so apparent to him that all other waves required media for their propagation, that the existence of a medium, pervading the whole of space, was postulated. This was named the *luminiferous ether*, and much ingenuity was exercised in tracking down its properties. Eventually, following the classic experiment of Michelson and Morley in 1887 and the subsequent development of relativity theory, it was possible to dispense with the concept of the ether; the modern physicist now not only accepts the idea of electromagnetic waves travelling through a vacuum, but also describes them in the same mathematical way as other waves.

1.2   Description of some of the waves we shall study

1.2.1   *Waves in strings*

In this section we shall deal briefly, and in a general way, with the different types of waves we shall meet later on in this book. We have already mentioned waves in strings, which are particularly suitable for study in that they exemplify many of the principles common to other types of wave in a way very easy to visualize. So, although these waves can hardly be said to be of central importance in physics, the principles involved certainly are.

Waves in strings may be either *transverse* or *longitudinal*. For a *transverse* wave, the direction of travel (or propagation direction) is at right angles to the disturbance. Let us imagine that a string is stretched horizontally, and that one end is agitated with an up-and-down movement; then we would have a transverse wave with disturbance in the up-and-down direction moving along the length of the string. At a given instant, the string might appear as in Figure 1(a). On the

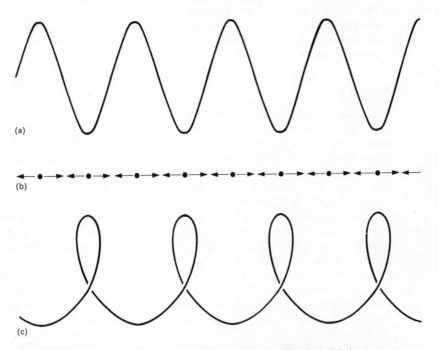

(a)

(b)

(c)

Figure 1 Sketches of profiles of three different waves on a string. (a) A transverse wave. Displacements are vertical. (b) A longitudinal wave. Arrows indicate the displacements at different parts of the string. (c) A perspective sketch of a circularly polarized wave. The wave is basically transverse since the displacements are everywhere at right angles to the direction of propagation

other hand, a *longitudinal* wave can be set up by taking one end of the string and successively stretching and releasing it along its own length. In this type of wave, the disturbance is in the direction of propagation, as illustrated in Figure 1(b).

Transverse and longitudinal waves have many properties in common with each other, as mathematical analyses later on in this book will show. But there is one great difference. When we specify a longitudinal wave, we know that the displacements of the particles in the cord (or whatever medium is sustaining the wave) are parallel to the direction of propagation. However, in the case of a transverse wave we have to specify not only the transverse nature of the wave motion but also the direction of the transverse displacement, since no particular perpendicular displacement is to be preferred to any other. For example, if the horizontally-stretched clothes line is displaced in either the vertical direction or the horizontal direction perpendicular to its length, a transverse wave will result. In fact, two transverse waves with different directions of displacement can be propagated at the same time along the cord; a particularly simple wave of this sort may be obtained by rotating one end of the clothes line in a circle whose plane is perpendicular to the length of the cord. In this case a wave is produced whose profile is illustrated in Figure 1(c). This is usually called a *circularly polarized wave*.

1.2.2   *Waves in rods*

Solid rods are capable of sustaining three different types of wave. The first and simplest is the longitudinal wave which is propagated because of the tensile elastic properties of the rod. It is quite easy to excite such waves. If a rod of length about one metre is held firmly at its centre and stroked along its length by a resined cloth, a longitudinal wave is propagated back and forth along the rod. It cannot be visually observed, but the effect of the wave can easily be audibly observed as a high-pitched sound of considerable purity. Because the rod is of comparatively small length, the *reflection* of the waves back along the rod when they reach either end becomes very important and determines the pitch of the note heard. We shall be dealing in detail with the phenomena of reflection in Chapter 5.

Transverse waves may exist in rods, but are more difficult to produce. They are mathematically much more complicated to analyse because, unlike either type of wave which exists on strings, different frequencies are propagated with different velocities. This is a phenomenon known as *dispersion* and will be studied in Chapter 7.

Finally, *torsional* waves may exist in rods. If a rod is twisted at one end, then the restoring torque causes a wave to be propagated. Here the 'disturbance' is not a linear displacement, but an angular twist. These waves are non-dispersive, that is, all frequencies are propagated at the same speed.

1.2.3   *Waves on membranes*

A membrane, for example the stretched skin on a drum, is the two-dimensional equivalent of a stretched string. Here, as in the string, when any part of the skin is pushed in a direction perpendicular to its plane and then released, transverse waves are set up. These waves, unlike those on the string, are two-dimensional – they spread out from the point of the initial disturbance in a way very similar to that in which surface waves on water spread out from a point of disturbance.

The simplest type of two-dimensional wave from the point of view of mathematical analysis is a 'straight-line' wave – one whose direction of propagation is constant over the whole surface and whose profile is the same along any line drawn in this direction. In general, the analysis of two-dimensional waves is not so simple, and indeed waves on a drum-head, which are reflected to the centre of the head when they reach the perimeter, require considerable sophistication for their analysis, which is outside the scope of this book.

2.4 *Sound waves*

We shall be discussing sound waves in considerable detail later on in the book. At this stage, we shall merely say that when a disturbance is created at some point, waves proceed from this point in all directions. Sound waves in gases are longitudinal because a gas is unable to sustain a torsional or shear force.

2.5 *Waves in transmission lines*

We turn back, now, to a one-dimensional example of wave motion, and one that is of great importance in certain electrical applications. An extreme convenience of electricity, as opposed to other forms of power, is that it can be conducted along metal wires to a point remote from the generator with the greatest ease. Normally, at least two parallel wires, or some similar arrangement such as coaxial wires, are required for this. There will thus be a small capacitance, and also inductance, between the wires which will cause, as we shall see in Chapter 4, a wave of voltage (and current) to travel along the line when the generator is delivering any voltage other than a perfectly steady d.c. The result of this is that the device at the end of the line remote from the generator does not 'see' the voltage variations at the generator, but a version of these as modified by the line. This can pose problems at high frequencies, but at lower frequencies, for example the 50 Hz mains, the effects of such modifications are utterly negligible.

2.6 *Waveguides*

Point sources of waves propagating into a three-dimensional medium produce spherical waves radiating outwards from the source at the centre. This means that a detector placed at successively greater distances from the source records successively weaker responses since the total flux of energy in the wave, which is constant, is being spread over the surface of a sphere of ever increasing surface area. This limits the effective range over which the detector can operate. In the case of sound waves, the point source would be reasonably well represented, several metres away, by a small loudspeaker, and the detector by a microphone or the ear. To increase the range it is possible to 'guide' the wave through a tube of constant internal size and shape so that the energy in the wave is not being wasted in detectorless regions. An obvious example of this arrangement, which is technically known as a *waveguide*, is the speaking tube. Other types of waveguide exist, notably the electromagnetic waveguide whose use overcomes some of the difficulties of transmitting high-frequency electrical signals along transmission lines; this type of waveguide will not, however, be discussed further in this book.

1.2.7 *Wave mechanics*

Finally, in this brief general look at waves, we come to a highly important example in atomic physics, to which the final chapter is devoted. It has been said that waves form a means of transmitting energy from one point in space to another without any matter being transmitted. This is in complete contrast to the rather more direct method of transmitting energy by propelling a particle between the two points in question. However, are the two situations so different?

Theoretical studies by de Broglie, followed by the discovery, by Davisson and Germer, of electron diffraction, showed that we must regard a particle in motion as a travelling wave. This is true for *all* particles, although the effects of the wave become important only for particles of atomic and subatomic size. The nature of the wave, and some of the consequences of assuming that the dynamics of masses are determined by the properties of a wave, will be investigated in Chapter 10.

Chapter 2
The Theory of Vibrations

1   The importance of vibration theory in the understanding of waves

When a medium is disturbed by the passage of a wave through it, the particles comprising the medium are caused to vibrate. To take a simple example, corks floating on the surface of a pond will bob up and down due to the influence of water waves. As will be seen later, the physical characteristics which describe a wave can be determined by observing the manner in which a particle in the path of the wave vibrates, so it is important at the outset to learn something of the nature and theory of vibrations.

2   Vibrations of a single particle

2.1   *Periodic motion of a point whose position is determined by a single variable*

Vibrating particles are the frequent concern of writers on mechanics; the bob of a simple pendulum and the weight hanging freely from the end of a spring are obvious examples of particles which may be set in vibration, and most people will have a good mental picture of how these vibrate. The motion is *periodic*; that is, after equal intervals of time (the *period* τ) the system finds itself in exactly the same situation. The bob of the pendulum, for example, is found to be at the same position, moving with the same velocity and acceleration as it was τ seconds earlier, and all these quantities will be the same τ, 2τ, 3τ, etc. seconds later. Actually the swings of a pendulum die away in time, due to frictional and viscous forces, but we are assuming an ideal pendulum which does not lose energy and goes on *ad infinitum*. During the interval of one period, a vibrating system is said to go through a *cycle* of situations, and the *frequency* (f) is defined as the number of cycles occurring in one second. Clearly, then, $f = 1/\tau$; the dimension of f is $[f] = [T^{-1}]$, so the unit of f is second^{-1}. This unit is termed the hertz.

The simplest kind of periodic motion is that experienced by a point, moving along a straight line, whose acceleration is directed towards a fixed point on the line and is proportional to its distance from the fixed point; this is called simple harmonic motion.

Let us take the one-dimensional case; that is, a moving point P moves along a straight line so that its position with respect to a fixed point O is completely specified by the single coordinate x. Let us examine the situation when the moving point is at P (position x) and moving away from O. The acceleration is d^2x/dt^2; this is directed towards O and proportional to the distance OP $= x$. Thus

$$\frac{d^2x}{dt^2} = -px,$$

where p is a positive constant.

Note the minus sign; this is because the acceleration is directed in the opposite direction to that in which x is increasing.

On rearranging, this equation becomes

$$\frac{d^2x}{dt^2} + px = 0. \qquad\qquad 2.1$$

This is a linear, second-order differential equation; linear because x and its derivative appear to the power one only, and second order because the highest derivative is d^2x/dt^2. Equation **2.1** is referred to as the differential equation governing the motion. It is not the equation of motion. To find the equation of motion we have to solve **2.1** for x. It can be shown (see for example H. T. H. Piaggio, *Differential Equations*, Bell, 1965) that the most general solution is

$$x = a\sin[(\sqrt{p})t + \epsilon]. \qquad\qquad 2.2$$

The two arbitrary constants, inevitable in the solution of any second-order differential equation, are, in this example, a and ϵ. That **2.2** is a solution of **2.1** can very easily be shown by differentiating **2.2** twice and substituting for x and d^2x/dt^2 in **2.1**.

The constant a is the *amplitude* of the motion; it is the greatest possible value that x can have, since the maximum value of $\sin[(\sqrt{p})t + \epsilon]$ is unity. Thus the motion takes place entirely between the limits $x = \pm a$. The quantity $(\sqrt{p})t + \epsilon$ is known as the *phase* of the motion; it tells us where the point is at any time;

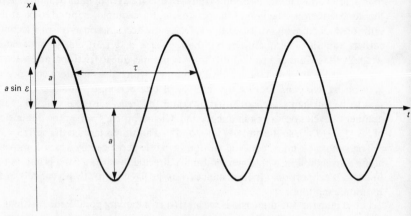

Figure 2 Plot of x against t for simple harmonic motion

ϵ is known as the *epoch* and it gives the position of the point at the instant $t = 0$, as shown in Figure 2, which is a plot of x against t. Clearly, when $t = 0$,

$$x = a \sin \epsilon.$$

Also shown in Figure 2 is the period τ; if we add τ to t in **2.2** the value of x must remain unaltered. Hence

$$x = a\sin[(\sqrt{p})t + \epsilon] = a\sin[\sqrt{p}(t + \tau) + \epsilon]. \qquad \textbf{2.3}$$

The smallest quantity we can add to the phase of **2.3** which leaves x unaltered for all values of t is 2π radians, or $360°$. Thus

$$\sqrt{p}\tau = 2\pi$$

and $\quad \sqrt{p} = \dfrac{2\pi}{\tau} = 2\pi f,$

since we saw earlier that the frequency $f = 1/\tau$. Thus we have found a physical meaning for p, and we can write the equation of motion in physically meaningful terms as

$$x = a\sin(2\pi ft + \epsilon). \qquad \textbf{2.4}$$

The product $2\pi f$ is sometimes replaced by the single quantity ω, which is known as the *angular frequency* or *pulsatance* of the motion.

In any given problem, the constants of integration a and ϵ are determined from the initial conditions. Suppose we are told that, at $t = t_0$ seconds, the point is x_0 metres from the origin and is moving with a velocity v_0 ms^{-1}. If we substitute these values into equation **2.4**, and the first derivative of **2.4**, we get

$$x_0 = a\sin(2\pi ft_0 + \epsilon) \qquad \textbf{2.5}$$

and $\quad v_0 = 2\pi fa\cos(2\pi ft_0 + \epsilon). \qquad \textbf{2.6}$

We can now solve for a and ϵ; firstly we divide **2.5** by **2.6** and invert the resulting tangent to get

$$\epsilon = \tan^{-1}\left(\frac{2\pi fx_0}{v_0}\right) - 2\pi ft_0.$$

Secondly we square and add the equations, using the identity

$$\cos^2\theta + \sin^2\theta = 1,$$

to get $\quad a^2 = x_0^2 + \dfrac{v_0^2}{4\pi^2 f^2}.$

There are numerous situations in physics which can be treated to a very good approximation as involving simple harmonic motion; we shall develop just two, one mechanical and one electrical.

Our mechanical example is that of a mass suspended from one end of an elastic string, the other end of which is rigidly clamped (Figure 3). Suppose the

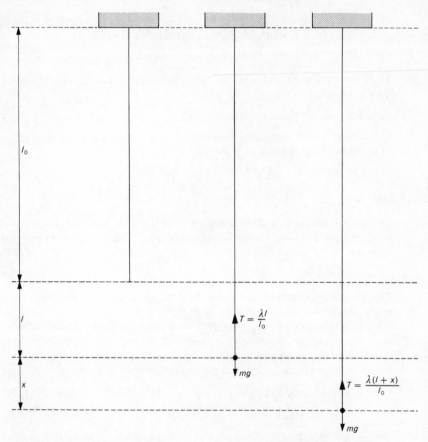

Figure 3 Motion of a mass suspended from a light, elastic string. (a) String hanging freely. (b) String with mass m suspended from end. (c) Mass in oscillation, at the instant when it is a distance x below equilibrium position

string is light, has an unstretched length l_0 and an elastic constant λ; when a mass m is hung from the end and lowered slowly to the equilibrium position, the string will be stretched a distance l such that, by Hooke's law

$$mg = \frac{\lambda l}{l_0},$$ **2.7**

where g is the acceleration due to gravity. Since λ and l_0 are both constants for a given string, we can replace λ/l_0 by the single constant k, which is known as the 'stiffness' of the string; so **2.7** becomes

$$mg = kl.$$ **2.8**

The dimensions of k are

$$[k] = [MLT^{-2}][L^{-1}] = [MT^{-2}].$$

If the mass is pulled down a small distance from the equilibrium position and released, vertical oscillations will ensue. Applying Newton's second law of motion (i.e. equating mass times acceleration to net force) to the situation shown in Figure 3(c), when the mass is instantaneously a distance x below the equilibrium position, we have

$$m\,\frac{d^2x}{dt^2} = mg - k(l + x).$$

But since $mg = kl$

(equation **2.8**), this becomes

$$m\,\frac{d^2x}{dt^2} = -kx$$

or $\quad m\,\dfrac{d^2x}{dt^2} + kx = 0.$ **2.9**

This has exactly the same form as equation **2.1**, so we can write down the general solution of **2.9**, as

$$x = a\sin\left(2\pi \sqrt{\left[\frac{k}{m}\right]}\, t + \epsilon \right),$$

which is the equation of motion of the mass. Thus the mass performs simple harmonic oscillations with period

$$\tau = 2\pi \sqrt{\left(\frac{m}{k}\right)} :$$

the constants a and ϵ could be determined from initial conditions (i.e. from a knowledge of the position x and the velocity dx/dt at some given time) as explained earlier.

The electrical example is that of the circuit shown in Figure 4 which comprises a capacitor of capacitance C in series with a coil of pure inductance L. The capacitor is charged from a battery, which is then removed, and the key K closed. The capacitor will thereupon discharge through the coil. Suppose, at some instant subsequent to the closing of the key, the charge on the capacitor is q and the current flowing through the coil is i; then the potential difference across the capacitor will be q/C and that across the coil $-L\,di/dt$. These must be equal; therefore, since

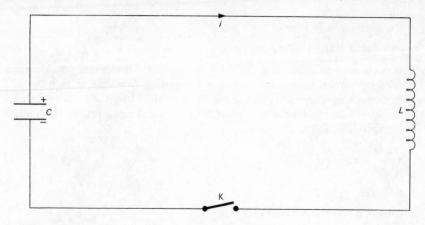

Figure 4 Circuit containing inductance and capacitance

$$i = \frac{dq}{dt},$$

we have $\quad L\,\dfrac{d^2q}{dt^2} + \dfrac{q}{C} = 0.$ **2.10**

The charge on the capacitor thus fluctuates with time according to the solution of **2.10**, which is

$$q = q_0 \sin\left(\frac{2\pi}{\sqrt{(LC)}}\,t + \epsilon\right).$$ **2.11**

As before, q_0 and ϵ could be determined from the initial conditions. According to **2.11** the charge on the capacitor would go on oscillating indefinitely. Experimentally, the charge would die away with time, just as the oscillations of the mass on the end of the string would die away. The dissipative effects of resistance, in the electrical case, and friction and viscosity, in the mechanical case, all of which have been ignored in our treatment, would cause the vibrations to lose energy and hence die away. It is not difficult to extend the theory to take account of these dissipative (or damping) effects, but we will not do so here.

2.2.2 *Periodic motion of a point in two dimensions*

Suppose a point is subjected simultaneously to two simple harmonic motions at right angles to one another. A physical example of this is the motion of the spot on a cathode-ray oscilloscope screen when alternating voltages are applied simultaneously to the X- and Y-plates.

Suppose that the voltage across the X-plates causes the spot to move according to the equation

$$x = a \sin 2\pi ft, \qquad\qquad\qquad 2.12$$

and that across the Y-plates causes the spot to move according to the equation

$$y = b \sin(2\pi ft + \epsilon). \qquad\qquad\qquad 2.13$$

This means that the alternating voltages have the same frequency f, different amplitudes, and differ in phase by ϵ radians. When the voltages are simultaneously applied, we can find the path described by the spot by eliminating the time t from equations **2.12** and **2.13** as follows. Expanding **2.13** we get

$$y = b \sin 2\pi ft \cos \epsilon + b \cos 2\pi ft \sin \epsilon. \qquad\qquad\qquad 2.14$$

From equation **2.12** we see that

$$\sin 2\pi ft = \frac{x}{a},$$

so that $\quad \cos 2\pi ft = \sqrt{\left(1 - \frac{x^2}{a^2}\right)}.$

Inserting these values into **2.14** and simplifying, we obtain

$$a^2 y^2 + b^2 x^2 - 2abxy \cos \epsilon - a^2 b^2 \sin^2\epsilon = 0. \qquad\qquad 2.15$$

Readers with a knowledge of conic sections will recognize this as the general equation for an ellipse. The form can readily be determined, and the curve sketched, by putting specific values of x and y into **2.15** as follows.

When
$y = 0$	$x = \pm a \sin \epsilon,$
$x = 0$	$y = \pm b \sin \epsilon,$
$x = \pm a$	$y = \pm b \cos \epsilon,$
$y = \pm b$	$x = \pm a \cos \epsilon.$

These points are plotted to give the curve shown in Figure 5.

Thus the picture we see on the screen will, in general, be an ellipse, and it is worth noting that the phase angle ϵ can be determined from it since

$$\frac{OA}{OB} = \sin \epsilon.$$

For special values of ϵ ($\epsilon = 0$ and π) the ellipse degenerates into a straight line, whilst for $\epsilon = \frac{1}{2}\pi$ and $\frac{3}{2}\pi$ the major and minor axes of the ellipse coincide with the X- and Y-axes. These particular instances are shown in Figure 6. The situation shown in Figure 6(a) could have easily been predicted; since the X- and

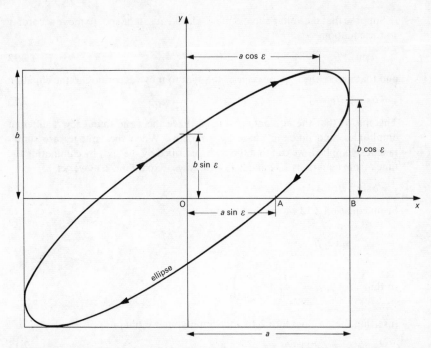

Figure 5 Two simple harmonic motions, of equal frequency, at right angles

Y-motions are in phase with one another, the maximum of X will occur at the same instant as the maximum of Y. The situation shown in Figure 6(b) for $\epsilon = \frac{1}{2}\pi$ [and Figure 6(d) for $\frac{3}{2}\pi$] is also of interest. If $a = b$ we have a circular path; this point will be pursued further during the discussion of polarization in Chapter 9.

The curves in Figure 6 are examples of what are known as Lissajous' figures. If the frequencies of the two signals are not the same, the figures become more complicated and are not, in general, stationary except when the frequencies are in the ratio of whole numbers.

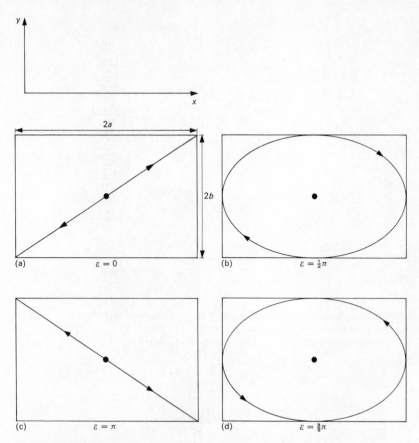

Figure 6 Special cases of simple harmonic motions at right angles

2.3 Vibrations of two coupled particles: Normal modes

We now need to investigate systems consisting of two particles coupled together. Examples of the types of system we have in mind are shown in Figure 7.

Eventually we shall obtain equations of motion of the masses shown in Figure 7(c), but before we embark on the mathematics it is very important that the reader should obtain a clear picture of the ways in which the particles in such systems can vibrate, so we strongly recommend that anyone meeting this subject for the first time should try the following simple experiment. The apparatus required is a 'Slinky' spring (obtainable from any toy shop) and about a metre of the type of chain used to secure wash-basin stoppers. The spring is cut into halves; the upper ends are clamped at the same level, as shown in Figure 8, and the ends of the chain are connected to the lower ends of the springs.

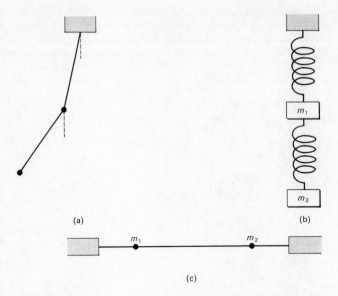

Figure 7 Systems with coupled particles. (a) Double pendulum.
(b) Two suspended masses and springs.
(c) Stretched elastic string, loaded with two masses

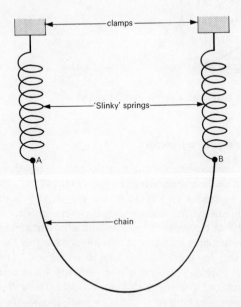

Figure 8 Spring-and-chain experiment to illustrate motion of a two-particle
system

The system so obtained is rather different from those shown in Figure 7, since it has a distributed mass rather than point masses. This makes the analysis much harder, but this does not matter since we do not intend to treat this system mathematically. We want to note how the positions of the points A and B, where the chain joins the springs, vary with time when the system is set into vertical motion.

Firstly, raise A and B by equal amounts and release them from rest. A and B should be seen to oscillate up and down with simple harmonic motion. Clearly A and B are exactly in phase – they are both at the top of the motion (or both at the bottom) at the same instant. Find an approximate value for the period. We will refer to this particular motion as mode 1.

Next lower A and raise B by equal amounts to the configuration shown in Figure 9(b) and release them from rest.

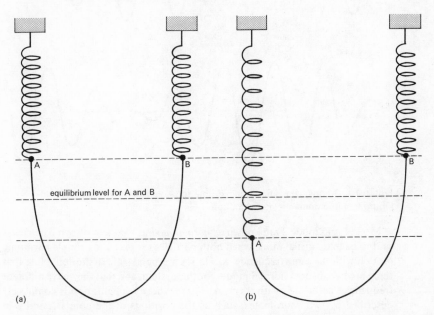

Figure 9 Starting positions of A and B for the two normal modes. (a) Mode 1. (b) Mode 2

Once more the points A and B should be seen to perform simple harmonic motion, but now in exact antiphase (A is at the top of its motion whilst B is at the bottom, and vice versa). We will refer to this motion as mode 2. Note that the period is not the same as for mode 1.

Bring the system to rest once more, and start motion by drawing A, alone, down and releasing it. The motion which follows (mode 3) should be seen to be of a much more complicated character than previously; neither A nor B oscillates with simple harmonic motion, but the variation of the position of each with time should be somewhat as shown in Figure 10. Note that the oscillations of both points successively build up and die away, and that A is oscillating with its greatest amplitude when B has minimum amplitude and vice versa. The kinetic energy of the system is, in fact, being periodically transferred from one side to the other.

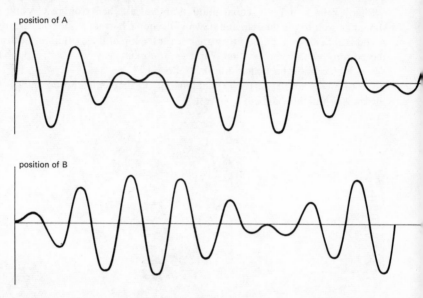

Figure 10 Graphs of position against time for A and B when the system of Figure 9 is in a general state of motion

Mode 1 and mode 2 are known as *normal modes*; a system of two particles is said to be in a normal mode when both particles are executing simple harmonic motion with the same frequency. Mode 3 is a general state of motion. Note that there are two distinct normal modes for this system, and that they have different frequencies associated with them. A system whose configuration is completely described by two coordinates, such as the positions of the points A and B in our example, is said to have two *degrees of freedom*. Such a system has two distinct normal modes of vibration. Note that it is incorrect in general to equate the number of degrees of freedom to the number of particles, since any particle may have up to three degrees of freedom. In our example the points A and B move up and down only, so the position of each is completely specified by a single coordinate.

Now that the reader has a qualitative idea of the way in which a system with two particles vibrates, the time has come to provide a proper quantitative analysis of the problem. We will take the system of Figure 7(c), a stretched light elastic string fixed at both ends and loaded with two equal masses; it will be seen later why this choice is an appropriate one for a book on waves. Let us assume that such a system has been set in motion, and that at a given instant the two masses are displaced transversely, as shown in Figure 11.

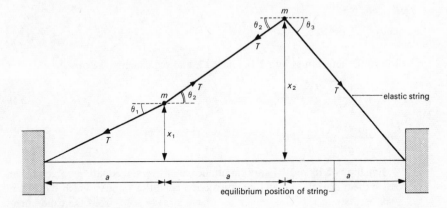

Figure 11 Loaded elastic string at some instant during motion

The following assumptions are made:

(a) The displacements x_1 and x_2 of the masses from their equilibrium positions are always small in comparison with the length of the string.

(b) The changes in the original tension T due to these small displacements can be ignored in comparison with T itself.

(c) The effects of gravity are ignored.

(d) The masses are equal and are at the points of trisection of the string, which is of length $3a$.

To obtain the differential equations governing the motions of the particles, we apply Newton's second law of motion. For the first mass,

$$m \frac{d^2 x_1}{dt^2} = T \sin \theta_2 - T \sin \theta_1,$$

which, when we replace $d^2 x_1/dt^2$ by $\ddot{x}_1$ for brevity, becomes

$$m\ddot{x}_1 = T \sin \theta_2 - T \sin \theta_1, \qquad\qquad \textbf{2.16}$$

and for the second mass

$$m\ddot{x}_2 = -T \sin \theta_2 - T \sin \theta_3; \qquad\qquad \textbf{2.17}$$

where the angles θ_1, θ_2, θ_3 are those shown in Figure 11.

Since x_1 is small,

$$\sin\theta_1 \simeq \tan\theta_1 = \frac{x_1}{a} \ ;$$

similarly $\quad \sin\theta_2 \simeq \dfrac{x_2 - x_1}{a}$

and $\quad \sin\theta_3 \simeq \dfrac{x_2}{a}.$

Inserting these values into **2.16** and **2.17**, and rearranging, we obtain

$$m\ddot{x}_1 + \frac{2Tx_1}{a} - \frac{Tx_2}{a} = 0, \qquad\qquad\qquad \textbf{2.18}$$

$$m\ddot{x}_2 + \frac{2Tx_2}{a} - \frac{Tx_1}{a} = 0. \qquad\qquad\qquad \textbf{2.19}$$

Equations **2.18** and **2.19** are simultaneous differential equations. Rather than solve them directly, we will investigate the conditions under which the system will oscillate in a normal mode. We have already seen, from the experiment, that in a normal mode the particles execute simple harmonic motion with the same frequency; we can therefore write down the equations of motion for the two masses as

$$x_1 = A\sin 2\pi ft, \qquad\qquad\qquad\qquad\qquad \textbf{2.20}$$

$$x_2 = B\sin 2\pi ft. \qquad\qquad\qquad\qquad\qquad \textbf{2.21}$$

There is no need to include an epoch (for example the epoch ϵ in **2.2**) since, as we have seen, the particles will either be exactly in phase or exactly in antiphase; in the latter case, A and B will have opposite signs because

$$\sin(2\pi ft + \pi) = -\sin 2\pi ft.$$

Substituting from **2.20** and **2.21** into **2.18** and **2.19** we obtain, after cancelling out the trigonometric terms,

$$-mA(2\pi f)^2 + \frac{2TA}{a} - \frac{TB}{a} = 0 \qquad\qquad\qquad \textbf{2.22}$$

and $\quad -mB(2\pi f)^2 + \dfrac{2TB}{a} - \dfrac{TA}{a} = 0. \qquad\qquad\qquad \textbf{2.23}$

We can eliminate the ratio A/B between these equations to get

$$\left[-m(2\pi f)^2 + \frac{2T}{a} \right]^2 = \frac{T^2}{a^2} \ ;$$

so $\quad -m(2\pi f)^2 + \dfrac{2T}{a} = \pm \left(\dfrac{T}{a} \right).$

Thus, solving for $(2\pi f)^2$ we have

$$(2\pi f)^2 = \dfrac{T}{ma} \quad \text{or} \quad \dfrac{3T}{ma}.$$

Thus there are two different frequencies with which this system oscillates in a normal mode; these are

$$f_1 = \dfrac{1}{2\pi} \sqrt{\left(\dfrac{T}{ma} \right)} \qquad \qquad \textbf{2.24}$$

and $\quad f_2 = \dfrac{1}{2\pi} \sqrt{\left(\dfrac{3T}{ma} \right)}. \qquad \qquad \textbf{2.25}$

If we now substitute the value of f_1 into **2.22**, we get

$A = B.$

Thus, in this (the first) normal mode, the amplitudes of motion of the masses are the same, and the latter move in phase at all times; the vibration will therefore be as shown in Figure 12(a).

If we substitute f_2 into **2.22**, we get

$A = -B;$

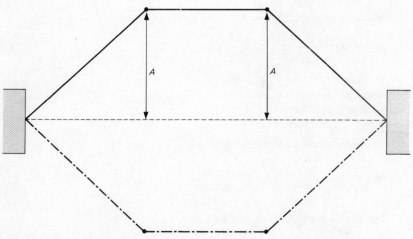

Figure 12 (a) The first normal mode

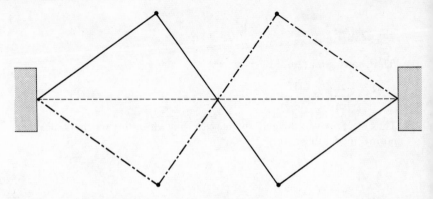

Figure 12 (b) The second normal mode

in the second normal mode, therefore, the amplitudes are the same but the motions are in antiphase, as indicated in Figure 12(b). The frequencies f_1 and f_2 corresponding to the normal modes are referred to as the *natural frequencies* of the system.

We must now find the equations of motion of the masses when the system is in a general state of motion. If we add together equations **2.18** and **2.19** we obtain

$$m(\ddot{x}_1 + \ddot{x}_2) + \frac{2T}{a}(x_1 + x_2) - \frac{T}{a}(x_1 + x_2) = 0, \qquad \textbf{2.26}$$

and if we subtract them we get

$$m(\ddot{x}_1 - \ddot{x}_2) + \frac{2T}{a}(x_1 - x_2) + \frac{T}{a}(x_1 - x_2) = 0. \qquad \textbf{2.27}$$

Writing $x_1 + x_2 = u$ in **2.26**
and $x_1 - x_2 = v$ in **2.27**,
so that $\ddot{x}_1 + \ddot{x}_2 = \ddot{u}$
and $\ddot{x}_1 - \ddot{x}_2 = \ddot{v}$,

we find that these equations simplify to

$$m\ddot{u} + \frac{T}{a}u = 0,$$

$$m\ddot{v} + \frac{3T}{a}v = 0.$$

These we recognize as the differential equations for simple harmonic motion (see **2.1**), so we can immediately write down their solutions (see **2.2**) as follows:

$$u = x_1 + x_2 = C \sin \left\{ 2\pi \sqrt{\left(\frac{T}{ma}\right)} \, t + \alpha \right\}$$

$$\text{and} \quad v = x_1 - x_2 = D \sin \left\{ 2\pi \sqrt{\left(\frac{3T}{ma}\right)} \, t + \beta \right\},$$

where C, D, α and β are the arbitrary constants of integration. We can solve for x_1 and x_2 as follows:

$$x_1 = \frac{u + v}{2}$$

$$= \tfrac{1}{2}C \sin \left\{ 2\pi \sqrt{\left(\frac{T}{ma}\right)} \, t + \alpha \right\} + \tfrac{1}{2}D \sin \left\{ 2\pi \sqrt{\left(\frac{3T}{ma}\right)} \, t + \beta \right\} \qquad \textbf{2.28}$$

and

$$x_2 = \frac{u - v}{2}$$

$$= \tfrac{1}{2}C \sin \left\{ 2\pi \sqrt{\left(\frac{T}{ma}\right)} \, t + \alpha \right\} - \tfrac{1}{2}D \sin \left\{ 2\pi \sqrt{\left(\frac{3T}{ma}\right)} \, t + \beta \right\}. \qquad \textbf{2.29}$$

Equations **2.28** and **2.29** are the equations of motion of the masses when the system is in a general state of motion. It will be seen that the motion in each case is the sum of two simple harmonic terms, and that the frequencies of these simple harmonic terms are, respectively, the frequencies associated with the two normal modes in which the system is capable of oscillating. This last point can be checked by comparing the frequency terms in **2.28** and **2.29** with f_1 and f_2 in equations **2.24** and **2.25**. Mathematically, equations **2.28** and **2.29** are said to be *linear combinations* of the normal-mode solutions.

The type of motion obtained when a particle executes two simple harmonic motions of different frequencies simultaneously is known as *beats*. This is the effect shown in Figure 10. At certain times the two motions will be in step with one another, resulting in a large displacement; but since the frequencies are different they will gradually get out of step and will eventually tend to cancel each other out, then later they will get back into step and so on.

The phenomenon of beats is more usually associated with the combination of two collinear simple harmonic motions of nearly the same frequency. Suppose we have two such motions of the same amplitude a, but whose frequencies differ by a small amount Δf. On combining, we get

$$y = a \sin 2\pi f t + a \sin 2\pi (f + \Delta f)t.$$

Applying the well-known trigonometrical formula

$$\sin A + \sin B = 2 \sin \tfrac{1}{2}(A + B) \cos \tfrac{1}{2}(A - B),$$

we have

$$y = 2a \cos \left[2\pi \, \frac{\Delta f}{2} \, t \right] \sin \left[2\pi \left(f + \frac{\Delta f}{2} \right) t \right].$$

This can be written as

$$y = A \sin 2\pi \bar{f} t,$$

where $\quad A = 2a \cos 2\pi \dfrac{\Delta f}{2} t$

and $\bar{f}$ is the mean of the two original frequencies. The result is therefore similar to simple harmonic motion, except that the amplitude changes slowly with time.

Probably the best example of this is the note produced when two tuning forks of the same nominal frequency are struck simultaneously. This note is heard to build up and die away alternately with low frequency. Since the ear recognizes intensity but not phase, it is unable to distinguish between the maxima and minima of A, so the apparent frequency of the beats (the so-called beat frequency) is Δf (the difference between the individual frequencies of the forks).

2.4 Systems with more than two particles

Systems of more than two particles can be analysed along the lines of section 2.3, but the mathematics becomes rather cumbersome. A system comprising a stretched elastic string loaded with three evenly spaced equal masses can be shown to have three normal modes of vibration and three natural frequencies. The normal-mode situations are shown in Figure 13. For this system, the general equation of motion for any of the particles can also be shown to be a linear combination of the three normal-mode solutions.

Extending the pattern further, a system of N particles (each particle having one degree of freedom only) can be shown to have N normal modes of vibration and N natural frequencies, and the general state of motion is a linear combination of the N normal-mode solutions.

An important extension of these ideas is encountered in the vibrations of a stretched heavy string. Such a string can be regarded as a system comprising an infinite number of particles, and will have an infinite number of normal modes and natural frequencies. It is possible to analyse the behaviour of a vibrating string in this way, but it is much more convenient to regard the string as a continuous medium, and to treat the problem by means of waves, as is done in Chapter 4.

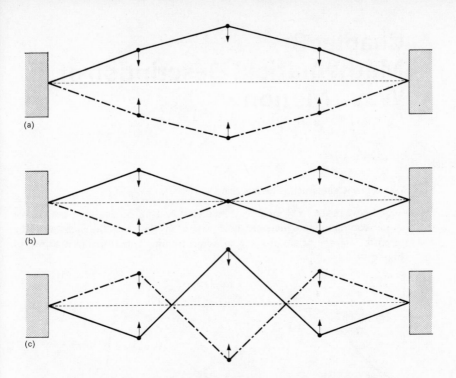

Figure 13 Normal modes for a three-particle system. (a) Mode 1 (lowest frequency). (b) Mode 2 (note that the central mass is permanently at rest). (c) Mode 3 (highest frequency)

Chapter 3
Mathematical Description of Wave Motion

3.1 Waves in one dimension: The function $y = f(x - ct)$

Suppose we have a very long horizontal elastic string, originally at rest. Let us choose coordinate axes such that the x-axis is along the string, the y-axis vertically upwards, and the origin at some convenient point. This situation is shown in Figure 14.

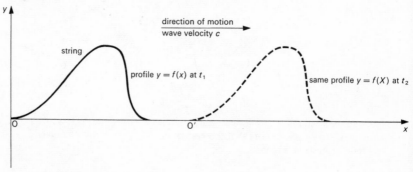

Figure 14 Waves on a long string

Suppose now that the string is set in motion by its being given a sudden flick at a point to the left of the origin. Experience tells us that this would result in a disturbance travelling down the string, the particles comprising the string being momentarily displaced from their original positions. Let us assume that this disturbance takes place parallel with the y-axis (i.e. that it is a true transverse wave) so that we may take the y-value of any point on the string as a measure of the disturbance of that point at a given instant of time. If a high-speed photograph is taken during the passage of the disturbance, the string will be seen to be distorted into a curve. This curve is referred to as the *wave profile*. We shall assume that this profile moves down the string with constant velocity c, and *without change of shape*. Thus if we take two photographs at times t_1 and t_2, both would show the same profile, but in the second photograph the profile would be displaced along the string in the direction of propagation. Let us describe the shape of the profile at time t_1 by the function

$$y = f(x).$$

On the second photograph, taken at time t_2, let us mark the point O′ on the x-axis which is at the same position relative to the profile as the origin O was in the photograph taken at time t_1. Let distance along the x-axis referred to O′ be measured by the quantity X. Thus the shape of the profile referred to O′ at time t_2 is

$$y = f(X).$$

It is obviously not convenient to have our origin of coordinates moving along with the profile; we want to refer the profile to the fixed point O. Now since the profile is moving with constant velocity c, the distance OO′ is $c(t_2 - t_1)$. Thus

$$X = x - c(t_2 - t_1).$$

The profile at time t_2 is then described by

$$y = f[x - c(t_2 - t_1)].$$

Finally, if our clock was started as the profile passed the point O, that is, $t_1 = 0$, then the profile at any subsequent time t is obtained by replacing the quantity $t_2 - t_1$ in this equation with the single quantity t, to give

$$y = f(x - ct). \tag{3.1}$$

This is an extremely important equation in the theory of wave motion. It completely defines a one-dimensional transverse wave of constant profile moving with constant velocity c along the positive direction of the x-axis. It is easy to show on the same lines, and it is left to the reader to do so, that a wave which is the same in all respects but moving in the opposite direction (i.e. along the direction of x decreasing) is given by

$$y = f(x + ct). \tag{3.2}$$

Equations **3.1** and **3.2** are examples of functions of two variables; to find y, we must know the values of the variables x and t (we must also know the form of the function f and the velocity c, but these do not change). Physically, this means that in order to find the disturbance suffered by a point on the string, we must specify not only its position along the string (x), but also the time (t) at which we wish to know the disturbance.

Equations **3.1** and **3.2** are not a really general description of wave motion in one dimension, in that two equations are required, one for each direction of propagation, and also because they are both specified in terms of a function f.

A completely general equation can be obtained by differentiating **3.1** (or **3.2**, for the result is the same for both) to eliminate from it all reference to the function f and the direction of propagation, as follows. In equation **3.1**, let us write

$$z = x - ct. \tag{3.3}$$

Then, differentiating $y = f(x - ct) = f(z)$ with respect to t, we obtain

$$\frac{\partial y}{\partial t} = \frac{df}{dz}\frac{\partial z}{\partial t}.$$

(The symbol ∂ indicates partial differentiation; for a full treatment of this subject see Chapter 1 of J. S. R. Chisholm and R. M. Morris, *Mathematical Methods in Physics*, North Holland, 1966. Note, however, the ds in df/dz since the function is one of z only.) But

$$\frac{\partial z}{\partial t} = -c \qquad \text{(from 3.3)}$$

and so $\quad \dfrac{\partial y}{\partial t} = -c\dfrac{df}{dz}.$ \hfill **3.4**

Similarly, $\quad \dfrac{\partial y}{\partial x} = \dfrac{df}{dz}\dfrac{\partial z}{\partial x},$

but, as $\quad \dfrac{\partial z}{\partial x} = 1, \qquad$ (from **3.3**),

we have $\quad \dfrac{\partial y}{\partial x} = \dfrac{df}{dz}.$ \hfill **3.5**

Eliminating df/dz between **3.4** and **3.5** we obtain

$$\frac{\partial y}{\partial t} = -c\frac{\partial y}{\partial x}.$$ \hfill **3.6**

Now we repeat the same process, but starting with $y = f(x + ct)$. Let $x + ct = w$; this leads to

$$\frac{\partial y}{\partial t} = +c\frac{df}{dw}$$ \hfill **3.7**

and $\quad \dfrac{\partial y}{\partial x} = \dfrac{df}{dw}.$ \hfill **3.8**

Eliminating df/dw between **3.7** and **3.8** gives

$$\frac{\partial y}{\partial t} = +c\frac{\partial y}{\partial x}.$$ \hfill **3.9**

We see that equations **3.6** and **3.9**, though very similar, are not identical; different results have been obtained for different directions of propagation. Let us see if we can eliminate all reference to direction of propagation by further differentiation. Differentiating **3.4** a second time with respect to t we have

$$\frac{\partial^2 y}{\partial t^2} = -c \frac{\partial}{\partial t} \left(\frac{df}{dz} \right)$$

$$= -c \frac{d}{dz} \left(\frac{df}{dz} \right) \frac{\partial z}{\partial t}.$$

But $\quad \dfrac{d}{dz} \left(\dfrac{df}{dz} \right) = \dfrac{d^2 f}{dz^2}$

and $\qquad \dfrac{\partial z}{\partial t} = -c \qquad$ (from **3.3**).

Therefore $\quad \dfrac{\partial^2 y}{\partial t^2} = c^2 \dfrac{d^2 f}{dz^2}.$ \hfill **3.10**

Similarly, differentiating **3.5** with respect to x leads to

$$\frac{\partial^2 y}{\partial x^2} = \frac{d^2 f}{dz^2}. \tag{3.11}$$

Finally, eliminating $d^2 f/dz^2$ between **3.10** and **3.11** gives

$$\frac{\partial^2 y}{\partial x^2} = \frac{1}{c^2} \frac{\partial^2 y}{\partial t^2}. \tag{3.12}$$

If we repeat the same process, starting with

$$y = f(x + ct),$$

we obtain precisely the same final result as **3.12**. This means that we have now obtained an equation which is completely independent of the direction of propagation. Equation **3.12** is an example of a *second-order partial differential equation*. The importance of this equation lies in its complete generality with regard to the form and direction of travel of waves which can be propagated in accordance with it. Examples of the occurrence of this equation in physics will be treated in the next chapter, and its solutions will be discussed in detail in Chapter 5.

.2 Harmonic waves

So far we have left the form of the function f in the equation

$$y = f(x - ct)$$

completely arbitrary. In other words, our wave profile may have the shape of any continuous curve. It turns out that the simplest wave to treat analytically is one whose profile is a pure sine curve. We can express such a wave as

$$y = f(x - ct) = a \sin b(x - ct),$$

3.13

where a and b are constants whose significances will appear shortly. Such a wave is known as a *sine wave*.

Suppose a wave described by equation **3.13** is propagated along a stretched elastic string of the kind described earlier in this chapter. How would a point on the string be disturbed due to the passage of the wave? We can answer this question by inserting the position of the point in question into **3.13**. Let its position be x_1 metres from the origin.

Hence $y = a \sin b(x_1 - ct)$

3.14

or $y = -a \sin b(ct - x_1).$

3.15

This equation tells us how the disturbance or transverse position y of the point varies with time t. Note that y is now a function of the single variable t, since x has been given the constant value x_1. Equation **3.14**, or **3.15**, is therefore the equation of motion of the point at $x = x_1$.

We saw, in Chapter 2, that a point executing simple harmonic motion has the equation of motion

$$y = a \sin(2\pi f t + \epsilon).$$

[2.4]

Comparing **2.4** with **3.15**, we see that these equations are really the same, except that the constants are differently arranged, so the point on the string will oscillate with simple harmonic motion. Furthermore, since we get the same form of equation **3.14** no matter what value of x is inserted, it follows that any point on the string along which a sine wave is propagated is caused to oscillate with simple harmonic motion. For this reason, sine waves are also referred to as *harmonic* waves.

A wave whose profile is that of a cosine function is very similar; sine and cosine functions have exactly the same form, the only difference between them being the point at which the origin is chosen. Since the choice of origin is always completely arbitrary, the first minus sign in **3.15** can be removed by a new choice of origin.

In order to get a complete picture of the motion of the point at $x = x_1$, we must compare corresponding terms in **3.15** and **2.4**. We can now identify the quantity a in **3.15** with the amplitude of the motion caused by the wave. The wave itself is said to have amplitude a.

Comparing **2.4** and **3.15** we see that

$$2\pi f = bc$$

or $b = \dfrac{2\pi f}{c} \cdot$

3.16

We thus have a physical meaning for b in terms of the frequency f of the oscillations caused by the wave, and of the wave velocity c. Further, since the period τ of a simple harmonic motion is $1/f$, we can identify the period of the wave as $2\pi/bc$.

If, for equation **3.13**, y is plotted against x for a given value of t (t_1 say), the curve shown in Figure 15 is obtained. Since the sine function is periodic, the wave profile repeats itself after fixed intervals of x. The repeat distance is known as the *wavelength* and is designated by λ.

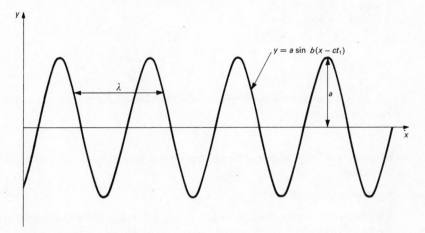

Figure 15 Graph of **3.13** for fixed t

If we increase x by λ in equation **3.16**, the value of y will, by definition, be unaltered,

i.e. $y = a \sin b(x - ct) = a \sin b(\overline{x + \lambda} - ct)$.

But the smallest quantity we can add into the phase of the sine function leaving it unaltered for all values of x is 2π. Hence

$$b\lambda = 2\pi$$

or $\quad b = \dfrac{2\pi}{\lambda}.$ **3.17**

From **3.16** and **3.17** we see that

$$b = \frac{2\pi}{\lambda} = \frac{2\pi f}{c},$$

which gives the extremely important result

$c = f\lambda.$ **3.18**

Thus the product of the frequency and the wavelength is equal to the velocity of the wave. We are now in a position to rewrite **3.13** in a number of equivalent forms,

$$y = a \sin \frac{2\pi}{\lambda}(x - ct),$$

$$y = a \sin 2\pi \left(\frac{x}{\lambda} - ft \right),$$

$$y = a \sin 2\pi \left(\frac{x}{\lambda} - \frac{t}{\tau} \right).$$

If we now define the *wave number k* as the number of wavelengths per metre, then $k = 1/\lambda$, and

$$y = a \sin 2\pi(kx - ft).$$

By a different initial choice of origin, we could equally well have arrived at the expression

$$y = a \sin 2\pi(ft - kx). \qquad \textbf{3.19}$$

Both representations of sine waves are commonly used, and they differ only in the choice of origin along the x-axis.

3.3   Exponential representation of a harmonic wave

It can be shown from the elementary theory of complex numbers that

$$\exp i\theta = \cos \theta + i \sin \theta, \qquad \textbf{3.20}$$

from which it follows that

$$\exp(-i\theta) = \cos \theta - i \sin \theta, \qquad \textbf{3.21}$$

where i is the imaginary quantity $\sqrt{(-1)}$. Here $\exp i\theta$ is a complex quantity, which is expressed as the sum of a real part, $\cos \theta$, and an imaginary part, $\sin \theta$. In this notation $\cos \theta$ may be referred to as the *real part* of $\exp i\theta$ – abbreviated to $\mathcal{R}(\exp i\theta)$, and $\sin \theta$ as the *imaginary part* of $\exp i\theta$ – abbreviated to $\mathcal{I}(\exp i\theta)$.

In this notation, equation **3.19** may be written as

$$y = a \sin 2\pi(ft - kx) = \mathcal{I}[a \exp 2\pi i(ft - kx)].$$

Finally, we drop the $\mathcal{I}$ from the written expression since it is always understood, when a sine wave is expressed in this form, that it is the imaginary part of the expression that has physical meaning. Thus,

$$y = a \exp 2\pi i(ft - kx). \qquad \textbf{3.22}$$

Similarly, when we wish to treat a cosine wave in this way, the real part of **3.22** is implied.

The advantage of this procedure is that exponentials are much easier to handle mathematically than sines and cosines; they are easier to integrate, differentiate and sum as series. The procedure is as follows. We express our sine (or cosine) waves in exponential form; then we carry out our manipulation and take the imaginary (or real) part of the result as the quantity which is physically meaningful.

That the exponential and trigonometrical treatments yield identical results is demonstrated in the following simple example of wave addition. Suppose we have two harmonic waves with identical amplitudes, frequencies and wave numbers moving in opposite directions;

$$y_1 = a \sin 2\pi(ft - kx)$$

and $y_2 = a \sin 2\pi(ft + kx).$

The sum of these is clearly

$$y = y_1 + y_2 = 2a \sin 2\pi ft \cos 2\pi kx. \qquad \textbf{3.23}$$

If we now express the two waves as exponentials (the imaginary part being tacitly understood), the sum is

$$y = a \exp 2\pi i(ft - kx) + a \exp 2\pi i(ft + kx),$$

which, on factorizing, becomes

$$y = a \exp 2\pi ift [\exp 2\pi ikx + \exp(-2\pi ikx)]. \qquad \textbf{3.24}$$

By eliminating $\sin \theta$ between **3.20** and **3.21** we see that

$$\cos \theta = \tfrac{1}{2}[\exp i\theta + \exp(-i\theta)].$$

Hence **3.24** becomes

$$y = 2a \exp 2\pi ift \cos 2\pi kx.$$

Finally, writing

$$\exp 2\pi ift = \cos 2\pi ft + i \sin 2\pi ft$$

(by **3.20**) and taking the imaginary part, we have

$$y = 2a \sin 2\pi ft \cos 2\pi kx,$$

which is the same as **3.23**. The reader will hardly gain the impression from this example that the exponential representation saves labour, but it does demonstrate that the correct result is obtained. Several further examples in this book will, however, bring home the usefulness of this approach. Finally, in adding two waves together we have anticipated some of the content of Chapter 5, where the physical significance of wave addition is discussed fully.

3.4   Waves in two and three dimensions: Wavefronts

3.4.1   *Two-dimensional waves: Straight-line wavefronts*

So far, we have confined our attention to waves in one-dimensional media, of which the stretched elastic string is an example. We must now extend our theory first to two, and finally three, dimensions. A convenient example of waves in a two-dimensional medium is that of water waves in, say, a ripple tank. Let us imagine that the surface of the water in the ripple tank has been disturbed, for example by dropping a long stick so that it enters the water horizontally. A disturbance will proceed along the surface in the form of a straight-line crest which, for the purpose of the present argument, we shall assume moves with constant velocity, and without change of shape, in directions perpendicular to the stick.

We shall need two Cartesian coordinates x and y to specify the position of a point on the surface of the water, and we shall designate the disturbance, which in this case is the vertical displacement of a point on the surface from its undisturbed position, by ϕ.

Figure 16 shows schematically what we would see on a high-speed photograph

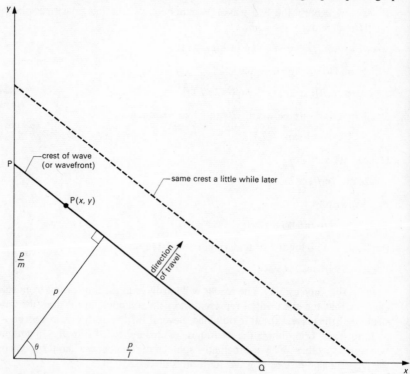

Figure 16 Straight-line water wave viewed from above

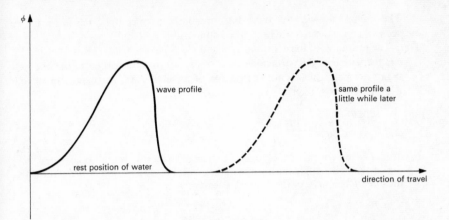

Figure 17 Vertical section through Figure 16 in the direction of travel of the wave

of such a system taken from above, whilst Figure 17 shows a vertical section in the direction in which the disturbance is travelling, which corresponds exactly to the one-dimensional wave we examined at the beginning of this chapter.

We meet now for the first time the concept of the wavefront; in the present case this is any continuous line joining points undergoing identical disturbance. Thus a crest is a wavefront, but so also is any other line joining points of equal disturbance. The importance of this concept resides in the fact that if we fix the state of disturbance as defining the wavefront, then the wavefront moves forward with the wave. In the present example the wavefront is a straight line, but we shall see later that this is not always the case.

We must now look for a way of describing waves propagated with constant velocity and shape in two dimensions, corresponding to $f(x - ct)$ for one-dimensional waves. What we do is to replace x in the one-dimensional equation by a quantity, containing both x and y, which is constant along a given wavefront. Suppose that a given wavefront has the instantaneous position given by the line PQ in Figure 16. Now any point along this line will satisfy the equation

$$lx + my = p,$$ **3.25**

where l, m and p are constants. [This is not the usual form of equation for a straight line used in coordinate geometry, but if we divide through by m and rearrange we get

$$y = \left(-\frac{l}{m} \right) x + \left(\frac{p}{m} \right),$$

which is now in the more usual form

$$y = Ax + B.$$

The reason why we have used this apparently more complicated form will be seen when we discuss waves in three dimensions.]

The meanings of the constants l, m and p will be seen from Figure 16. Clearly, p is the length of the perpendicular (or normal) from the origin to the line PQ. If this normal, which is in the direction of travel of the wave, makes an angle θ with the Ox axis, then

$$\cos \theta = l$$

and $\sin \theta = m$.

Thus l is the cosine of the angle the normal makes with the Ox axis and m is the cosine of the angle the normal makes with the Oy axis; l and m are known as the *direction cosines* of the normal. Clearly

$$l^2 + m^2 = 1.$$

Thus **3.25** expresses the equation of a straight line in terms of the direction cosines of the line normal and the perpendicular distance from the origin to the line.

Since the wave is travelling in the direction of p, and since the value of p is constant for a wavefront at a given time, the function $\phi = f(p - ct)$ is that which describes the wave. As

$$p = lx + my, \qquad\qquad\qquad\qquad\qquad\qquad\qquad\qquad\text{[3.25]}$$

we can write the wave function finally as

$$\phi = f(lx + my - ct). \qquad\qquad\qquad\qquad\qquad\qquad\textbf{3.26}$$

Thus **3.26** specifies a wave in two dimensions, of constant profile and constant velocity, with wavefronts which are straight lines, moving in the direction having direction cosines (l, m). Similarly it can be shown that

$$\phi = f(lx + my + ct)$$

represents a wave of identical profile moving in the opposite direction. If we eliminate the functional form f, and reference to the direction of propagation, from **3.26** by differentiation, along similar lines to the one-dimensional case, we obtain the partial differential equation

$$\frac{\partial^2 \phi}{\partial x^2} + \frac{\partial^2 \phi}{\partial y^2} = \frac{1}{c^2}\frac{\partial^2 \phi}{\partial t^2}. \qquad\qquad\qquad\qquad\textbf{3.27}$$

This is the partial differential equation governing straight-line wave propagation in two dimensions; but in fact it covers wavefronts of any shape.

3.4.2 *Two-dimensional harmonic waves: Vector representation*

A harmonic wave in two dimensions is typified by a water wave whose vertical section in the direction of travel is a sine curve. We may therefore mathematically describe such a wave, whose wavefronts are straight lines, by the equation

$$\phi = a\sin\frac{2\pi f}{c}(lx + my - ct).$$ 3.28

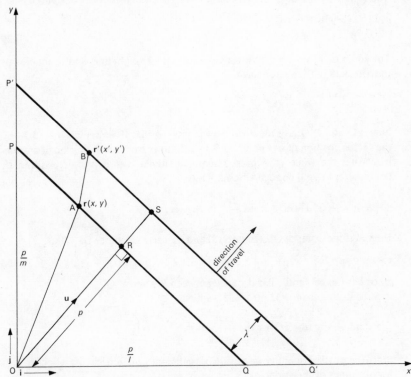

Figure 18 Vector representation of straight-line wave

The quantity $2\pi f/c$ is obtained by exactly the same process as that which led to equation **3.16** earlier in this chapter, whilst a represents the amplitude of the wave, as before. A high-speed photograph of water waves of this kind taken from above would be characterized by a family of equispaced parallel crests, the perpendicular distance between adjacent crests being the wavelength λ.

Two adjacent crests, PQ and P′Q′, are shown in Figure 18. (Actually PQ and P′Q′ need not be crests, but any pair of adjacent identical wavefronts.) Let us define unit vectors **i** and **j** parallel to Ox and Oy respectively, and let the unit vector along the direction of wave travel (i.e. the perpendicular to the wavefront) be **u** as shown. Take any point $A(x, y)$ with vector position **r** on the wavefront PQ; we can express the vector **r** in terms of its components as follows:

$$\mathbf{r} = x\mathbf{i} + y\mathbf{j}.$$

Similarly we can express the unit vector **u** as

$$\mathbf{u} = l\mathbf{i} + m\mathbf{j},$$

where l and m are the direction cosines of **u**. The scalar product of **r** and **u** is

$$\mathbf{r} \cdot \mathbf{u} = (x\mathbf{i} + y\mathbf{j}) \cdot (l\mathbf{i} + m\mathbf{j})$$
$$= lx + my = p. \tag{3.29}$$

The equation $\mathbf{r} \cdot \mathbf{u} = p$ is the vector equation for a straight line, and it enables us to write **3.28** in the vector form,

$$\phi = a \sin \frac{2\pi f}{c} (\mathbf{r} \cdot \mathbf{u} - ct). \tag{3.30}$$

Now PQ and P′Q′ are identical wavefronts, so that if we replace **r** in **3.30** by the vector position of *any* point on P′Q′ it follows from the definition of a wavefront that the value of ϕ must remain unaltered. Let B [vector position **r′**, coordinates (x', y')] be such a point. Thus

$$\phi = a \sin \frac{2\pi f}{c} (\mathbf{r} \cdot \mathbf{u} - ct) = a \sin \frac{2\pi f}{c} (\mathbf{r'} \cdot \mathbf{u} - ct). \tag{3.31}$$

But $\mathbf{r} \cdot \mathbf{u}$ is the distance OR (Figure 18) and $\mathbf{r'} \cdot \mathbf{u}$ is the distance OS. Thus

$$\mathbf{r'} \cdot \mathbf{u} - \mathbf{r} \cdot \mathbf{u} = \mathrm{RS} = \lambda, \tag{3.32}$$

since λ is the perpendicular distance between PQ and P′Q′.

Substituting from **3.32** into **3.31** we have

$$\phi = a \sin \frac{2\pi f}{c} (\mathbf{r} \cdot \mathbf{u} - ct) = a \sin \frac{2\pi f}{c} [(\mathbf{r} \cdot \mathbf{u} + \lambda) - ct].$$

Since the smallest quantity we can add into the sine function leaving it unchanged, for all values of the variables, is 2π, we have

$$\frac{2\pi f}{c} \lambda = 2\pi$$

and $\quad \lambda = \dfrac{c}{f}$,

as before, so we can rewrite **3.30** in the form

$$\phi = a \sin 2\pi \left(\frac{\mathbf{r} \cdot \mathbf{u}}{\lambda} - ft \right). \tag{3.33}$$

We now extend the earlier definition of the wave number k $(= 1/\lambda)$ so that it becomes the *wave vector* **k**. The direction of **k** is perpendicular to the wavefront (that is, parallel to the unit vector **u**) whilst the magnitude $|\mathbf{k}|$ is $1/\lambda$, as before. Hence

$$\frac{\mathbf{u}}{\lambda} = \mathbf{k}$$

and **3.33** becomes

$$\phi = a \sin 2\pi(\mathbf{k}\cdot\mathbf{r} - ft). \qquad\qquad \textbf{3.34}$$

This is the vector representation of a harmonic wave in its final form, though we can of course use the exponential form

$$\phi = a \exp 2\pi i(\mathbf{k}\cdot\mathbf{r} - ft). \qquad\qquad \textbf{3.35}$$

3.3 *Waves in three dimensions*

Equations **3.34** and **3.35** can be taken over, without change of form, into three dimensions. The three-dimensional equivalent of the straight line in two dimensions is the plane, so that the straight-line wavefronts of the previous section become plane wavefronts in three dimensions, and now **r** specifies a point in three-dimensional space.

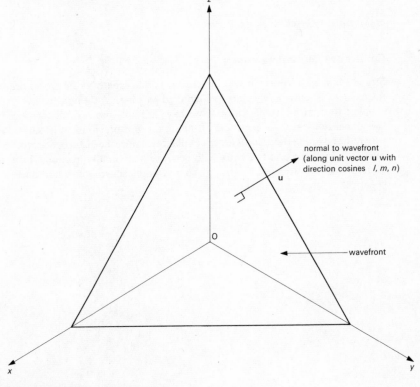

Figure 19 A plane wavefront

If we wish to specify a three-dimensional plane wave in Cartesian form, we can extend the two-dimensional equation **3.26** to

$$\phi = f(lx + my + nz - ct),$$ **3.36**

where (l, m, n) are the direction cosines of the normal to the plane wavefront (Figure 19). The partial differential equation, which is the three-dimensional equivalent of **3.27**, is

$$\frac{\partial^2 \phi}{\partial x^2} + \frac{\partial^2 \phi}{\partial y^2} + \frac{\partial^2 \phi}{\partial z^2} = \frac{1}{c^2} \frac{\partial^2 \phi}{\partial t^2},$$ **3.37**

which is easily verified by differentiating **3.36**.

It is convenient to write **3.37** in the form

$$\nabla^2 \phi = \frac{1}{c^2} \frac{\partial^2 \phi}{\partial t^2},$$

where ∇^2 (referred to in speech as 'del squared') is an abbreviation of

$$\left(\frac{\partial^2}{\partial x^2} + \frac{\partial^2}{\partial y^2} + \frac{\partial^2}{\partial z^2} \right),$$

and is often referred to as the Laplacian.

3.5   **Circular and spherical wavefronts**

Straight-line wavefronts (in two dimensions) and plane ones (in three) are by no means the only wavefronts encountered in physics, though they are the simplest to treat mathematically. If we have a point source of disturbance in two dimensions, such as a pebble dropping on to a previously still surface of water, the resulting wavefronts are of circular form since the disturbance proceeds outwards from the point of entry with equal velocity in all directions. In three dimensions, the wavefronts arising from a point source of disturbance are spherical in form.

Chapter 4
Waves in Physical Media

4.1 Introduction

In Chapter 3 we derived the partial differential equation governing wave propagation in one dimension,

$$\frac{\partial^2 y}{\partial x^2} = \frac{1}{c^2} \frac{\partial^2 y}{\partial t^2},$$

[3.12]

from purely geometrical considerations. We assumed a wave profile was being transmitted without change of shape and with constant velocity, but gave no physical justification for these assumptions. We will now look at some instances of wave propagation which will lead to equations of the type **3.12**.

4.2 Transverse wave in an infinitely long, stretched elastic string

Suppose our infinitely long elastic string is initially at rest (in equilibrium) and lies along the Ox axis of coordinates. We will measure the transverse disturbance due to the passage of the wave by y. Let the mass per unit length of string be μ and let the tension in the string be T.

We will make the following assumptions:

(a) The value of y is very small compared with any wavelength with which we are concerned, and

$$\frac{\partial y}{\partial x} \ll 1.$$

(b) There is no motion other than in the y-direction.

(c) The tension in the string is unaltered by the passage of the wave.

(d) The effects of gravity can be ignored; i.e. the weight of the string is left out of our considerations.

We now obtain the partial differential equation, governing the propagation of transverse waves along the string, by applying Newton's second law of motion to a short element of the string at an instant during the passage of the wave. We consider the motion of the element of length δx whose equilibrium position is PQ (Figure 20). At an instant during the passage of the wave, the element is displaced to the instantaneous position P'Q'.

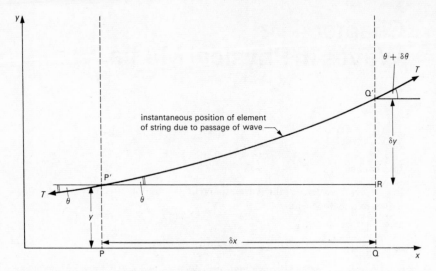

Figure 20 Element of string displaced by passage of wave

The angles made by the string with the Ox axis at the points P′ and Q′ are θ and $\theta + \delta\theta$ as shown in Figure 20; the only forces acting on the element are the tensions exerted by the adjoining sections of string at P′ and Q′. The net force acting in the Oy direction is therefore

$$T\sin(\theta + \delta\theta) - T\sin\theta.$$

Since the string always makes small angles with the Ox axis [assumption (a)], this becomes

$$T(\theta + \delta\theta) - T\theta = T\,\delta\theta$$

(where the angles are in radians). This can be rewritten as

$$T\frac{\partial\theta}{\partial x}\delta x. \qquad\qquad 4.1$$

Now in the triangle P′Q′R (Figure 20) we see that

$$\tan\theta = \frac{\delta y}{\delta x}.$$

But since θ is a small angle

$$\theta \simeq \tan\theta = \frac{\delta y}{\delta x}.$$

In the limit, as $\delta x \to 0$ we have, by definition,

$$\lim_{\substack{\delta x \to 0 \\ (t\,\text{constant})}} \frac{\delta y}{\delta x} = \frac{\partial y}{\partial x}.$$

Therefore $\quad \theta = \dfrac{\partial y}{\partial x}$

and $\qquad \dfrac{\partial \theta}{\partial x} = \dfrac{\partial^2 y}{\partial x^2}.$ **4.2**

Substituting for $\partial \theta / \partial x$ from **4.2** into **4.1** we have

Net force $= T \dfrac{\partial^2 y}{\partial x^2} \delta x.$ **4.3**

The rate of change of momentum of the element PQ is the product of the mass and the acceleration,

$$\mu \, \delta x \, \frac{\partial^2 y}{\partial t^2}.$$ **4.4**

Finally, equating **4.3** and **4.4** by Newton's second law of motion, and cancelling δx throughout, we have

$$\frac{\partial^2 y}{\partial x^2} = \frac{1}{T/\mu} \frac{\partial^2 y}{\partial t^2}.$$

This equation is in the same form as equation **3.12**, so we see at once, subject to all the assumptions we have made, that transverse waves of any profile can be propagated along a stretched elastic string, and that they will travel with the unique velocity $\sqrt{(T/\mu)}$. We can alter this velocity only by changing the tension or the density of the string (or both).

4.3 **Longitudinal waves in a fluid (liquid or gas)**

Suppose we have an infinitely long hollow tube (Figure 21), of circular cross-section of area A, containing a fluid (liquid or gas). Suppose that originally the fluid is at rest, its density is ρ_0 and the pressure is P_0. Consider the small cylinder of fluid of length δx between R and S, shown in Figure 21(a), originally at rest with an equal pressure P_0 exerted at both ends by the surrounding fluid. Suppose the fluid is set into longitudinal agitation, for example by inserting a piston in the tube somewhere to the left of R and causing it to oscillate axially. Clearly this will set the adjacent fluid into longitudinal oscillation, and this disturbance will pass along the fluid in the form of a longitudinal wave. Suppose that at a given instant the cylinder RS has become displaced to a new position such that R moves a distance z to R′ and S moves a distance $z + \delta z$ to S′. The variable z

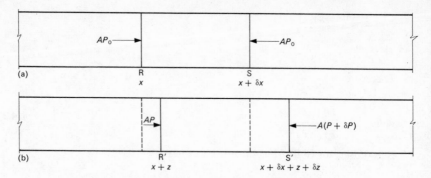

Figure 21 Waves in a fluid. In (a) the fluid is at rest in equilibrium, whilst in (b) the passing wave has displaced the cylinder RS to R'S'

measures the longitudinal displacement of a point due to the passage of the wave. Let the pressure on the left-hand face now be P and that on the right-hand face $P + \delta P$.

We derive the differential equation governing the propagation of longitudinal waves in two steps. First we relate the change in dimensions of the cylinder to the change in pressure; then we equate the rate of change of momentum of the cylinder to the force acting upon it, by Newton's second law of motion.

The relation between the change in pressure $P - P_0$ (which we will call the acoustic pressure p) and the fractional change in volume of the cylinder is

$$p = -K \frac{A \, \delta z}{A \, \delta x},$$

where K is the bulk modulus, since the original volume was $A \, \delta x$ and the increase in volume $A \, \delta z$. Here we have ignored δP in comparison with $P - P_0$; the minus sign arises because an increase in pressure is accompanied by a decrease in volume. In the limit, as $\delta x \to 0$, we have

$$p = -K \lim_{\delta x \to 0} \frac{\delta z}{\delta x} = -K \frac{\partial z}{\partial x}. \qquad \textbf{4.5}$$

Equating the net force on RS to the rate of change of momentum (product of mass and acceleration), we have

$$PA - A(P + \delta P) = A\rho_0 \, \delta x \, \frac{\partial^2 z}{\partial t^2}. \qquad \textbf{4.6}$$

We cannot ignore δP here, since it is this difference in pressure, however small, that is causing the motion. Now

$$p = P - P_0,$$

so $\quad \delta p = \delta P,$

since P_0 is constant; thus **4.6** becomes

$$-A \, \delta p = A\rho_0 \, \delta x \, \frac{\partial^2 z}{\partial t^2}.$$

We may write

$$\delta p = \frac{\partial p}{\partial x} \, \delta x,$$

since δx is small. Thus

$$-\frac{\partial p}{\partial x} \, \delta x = \rho_0 \, \delta x \, \frac{\partial^2 z}{\partial t^2}. \qquad\qquad \textbf{4.7}$$

Differentiating **4.5** with respect to x we see that

$$\frac{\partial p}{\partial x} = -K \, \frac{\partial^2 z}{\partial x^2};$$

substituting this into **4.7** we have

$$\frac{\partial^2 z}{\partial x^2} = \frac{1}{K/\rho_0} \, \frac{\partial^2 z}{\partial t^2}. \qquad\qquad \textbf{4.8}$$

Thus longitudinal waves may be propagated in a fluid and have a velocity of $\sqrt{(K/\rho_0)}$.

4.4 Pressure waves in a gas

The result **4.8** is not particularly useful, since we are not usually interested in how the longitudinal positions of points within the fluid vary due to the wave. On a molecular scale the position of a point in a fluid is a rather meaningless concept because, as the kinetic theory tells us, the molecules in a liquid or a gas are continuously moving about at very high velocities. What is of great importance is the variation of pressure due to waves in fluids – particularly gases. The partial differential equation governing pressure waves is obtained from equation **4.5**,

$$p = -K \, \frac{\partial z}{\partial x}. \qquad\qquad [\textbf{4.5}]$$

If we differentiate this equation twice partially with respect to time we get

$$\frac{\partial^2 p}{\partial t^2} = -K \, \frac{\partial^2}{\partial t^2} \left(\frac{\partial z}{\partial x} \right).$$

When we carry out the differentiation of the right-hand side, we obtain the so-called mixed derivative, which is written in the form

$$\frac{\partial^2}{\partial t^2}\left(\frac{\partial z}{\partial x}\right) = \frac{\partial^3 z}{\partial t^2 \partial x}. \qquad \textbf{4.9}$$

Note that the order in which the terms appear in the denominator of the right-hand side of **4.9** shows the order in which differentiation takes place. Thus

$$\frac{\partial^2 p}{\partial t^2} = -K\frac{\partial^3 z}{\partial t^2 \partial x}. \qquad \textbf{4.10}$$

Differentiating **4.5** partially with respect to x gives

$$\frac{\partial p}{\partial x} = -K\frac{\partial^2 z}{\partial x^2}. \qquad \textbf{4.11}$$

But
$$\frac{\partial^2 z}{\partial x^2} = \frac{1}{K/\rho_0}\frac{\partial^2 z}{\partial t^2}; \qquad \textbf{[4.8]}$$

eliminating $\partial^2 z/\partial x^2$ between **4.8** and **4.11**,

$$\frac{\partial p}{\partial x} = -\rho_0\frac{\partial^2 z}{\partial t^2},$$

and differentiating partially with respect to x again

$$\frac{\partial^2 p}{\partial x^2} = -\rho_0\frac{\partial}{\partial x}\left(\frac{\partial^2 z}{\partial t^2}\right) = -\rho_0\frac{\partial^3 z}{\partial x \partial t^2}. \qquad \textbf{4.12}$$

If we compare the derivatives on the right-hand sides of **4.10** and **4.12**, we see that the only difference between them is the order in which differentiation occurs. It turns out that, for all well-behaved mathematical functions of more than one variable, the order of differentiation in the mixed derivatives is immaterial, so we may write

$$\frac{\partial^3 z}{\partial t^2 \partial x} = \frac{\partial^3 z}{\partial x \partial t^2}.$$

We may almost invariably use this identity for functions which occur in physics. Eliminating this quantity between **4.10** and **4.12** we get

$$\frac{\partial^2 p}{\partial x^2} = \frac{1}{K/\rho_0}\frac{\partial^2 p}{\partial t^2},$$

so that the pressure waves have the same velocity, $\sqrt{(K/\rho_0)}$, as the displacement waves.

It turns out that, for an ideal gas, the conditions under which the pressure varies are adiabatic. An explanation of this is given on p. 62 of D. Tabor, *Gases, Liquids and Solids*, Penguin, 1969.

The behaviour of a fixed mass of ideal gas under adiabatic conditions is described by the equation

$$PV^\gamma = \text{constant},$$

where γ is the ratio c_P/c_V of the principal specific heats. Differentiating, we have

$$V \frac{dP}{dV} = -\gamma P.$$

But the bulk modulus

$$K = -V \frac{dP}{dV},$$

enabling us immediately to see that

$$K = \gamma P,$$

so that the velocity for sound waves in an ideal gas may be written

$$c = \sqrt{\left(\frac{\gamma P}{\rho_0} \right)}.$$

4.5   Longitudinal waves in a rod

The reasoning of the previous section can be applied with very little modification to the case of longitudinal waves in a rod. Consider the small section PQ of the

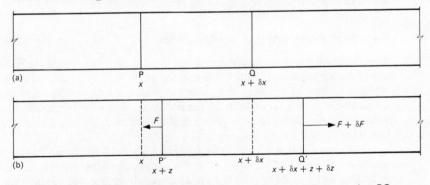

Figure 22 Longitudinal waves in a rod: (a) at rest, whilst in (b) the section PQ is displaced to P'Q' due to the passage of the wave

rod (Figure 22) of cross-sectional area A, made of material of density ρ and Young's modulus E; the section is displaced to P'Q', and is increased in length due to the passage of the longitudinal wave. Let the forces acting instantaneously on P'Q' be as shown in Figure 22(b).

Relating change in length to force acting, we have, from the definition of Young's modulus,

$$\frac{F}{A} = E \frac{\delta z}{\delta x},$$

4.13

ignoring δF in comparison with F. Applying Newton's second law of motion we have

$$\delta F = A\rho \, \delta x \, \frac{\partial^2 z}{\partial t^2}.$$

But

$$\delta F = \frac{\partial F}{\partial x} \delta x$$

$$= AE \frac{\partial^2 z}{\partial x^2} \delta x \qquad \text{by } \mathbf{4.13}.$$

Hence

$$\frac{\partial^2 z}{\partial x^2} = \frac{1}{E/\rho} \frac{\partial^2 z}{\partial t^2},$$

which is the wave equation once again. The velocity for longitudinal waves in a rod is thus

$$c = \sqrt{\frac{E}{\rho}}.$$

This gives velocities of the order of 5000 m s^{-1} when typical values of E and ρ for common metals are placed in this equation.

4.6 Current and voltage waves in a transmission line

A transmission line is a system of conductors (usually two) for carrying electrical energy from one point to another. The simplest example to treat mathematically is that of a pair of infinitely long, identical, parallel wires connected to the terminals of an alternating current generator, as shown in Figure 23. The generator causes fluctuations in voltage and current, which proceed along the line in the form of electrical waves.

We will investigate the changes that take place in a small section of the line of length δx between PP' and QQ'. We will assume that the wires have zero resistance, and that there is no leakage of current from one wire to the other. A line fulfilling these ideal conditions is said to be 'loss free'.

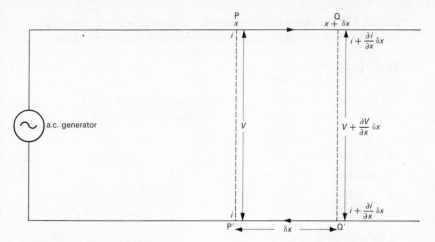

Figure 23 Ideal transmission line

A pair of wires of this kind acts as a capacitor (it can be thought of as a one-dimensional analogue of a parallel-plate capacitor). Let the capacitance per unit length be C. As the current will be changing with time, the magnetic flux produced by the current will also be changing so that we shall have an inductive effect. Let the inductance per unit length of the line be L.

For such a line, the currents at any opposite points (such as P and P′) must, at any instant, be the same in magnitude but opposite in direction. Let the various currents and potential differences at a given instant be as shown in Figure 23. Now the change in potential difference

$$\frac{\partial V}{\partial x} \delta x$$

between PP′ and QQ′ is due to the inductive effect, therefore

$$\frac{\partial V}{\partial x} \delta x = -\text{(the inductance of the element of length } \delta x) \times \frac{\partial i}{\partial t}.$$

Thus $\quad \dfrac{\partial V}{\partial x} \delta x = -L \dfrac{\partial i}{\partial t} \delta x,$

giving $\quad \dfrac{\partial V}{\partial x} = -L \dfrac{\partial i}{\partial t}$ **4.14**

(the minus sign appearing because the induced voltage always opposes the change in current producing it). The change in current

$$\frac{\partial i}{\partial x} \delta x$$

between PP′ and QQ′ is brought about by the capacitance effect. The amount of charge δq that accumulates in the section in a short time interval δt is

$$\delta q = -\left(\frac{\partial i}{\partial x}\,\delta x\right)\delta t. \qquad \textbf{4.15}$$

But the change of charge δq is accompanied by a change in potential δV, and these are related to the capacitance of the element as follows.

$$\delta q = (\text{total capacitance of element}) \times \delta V,$$

i.e. $\quad \delta q = (C\,\delta x)\,\delta V. \qquad \textbf{4.16}$

Combining **4.15** and **4.16**, we have

$$\frac{\partial i}{\partial x} = -C\frac{\delta V}{\delta t}.$$

In the limit, as $\delta t \to 0$,

$$\frac{\delta V}{\delta t} \to \frac{\partial V}{\partial t}$$

and $\quad \dfrac{\partial i}{\partial x} = -C\dfrac{\partial V}{\partial t}. \qquad \textbf{4.17}$

Differentiating **4.14** partially with respect to x gives

$$\frac{\partial^2 V}{\partial x^2} = -L\frac{\partial^2 i}{\partial t \partial x}, \qquad \textbf{4.18}$$

and differentiating partially **4.17** with respect to t gives

$$\frac{\partial^2 i}{\partial x \partial t} = -C\frac{\partial^2 V}{\partial t^2}. \qquad \textbf{4.19}$$

Equating the mixed derivatives, as in section 4.5, and eliminating them between **4.18** and **4.19** we obtain

$$\frac{\partial^2 V}{\partial x^2} = LC\frac{\partial^2 V}{\partial t^2}. \qquad \textbf{4.20}$$

Following almost the same procedure, but differentiating **4.14** with respect to t and **4.17** with respect to x, leads to the equation

$$\frac{\partial^2 i}{\partial x^2} = LC\frac{\partial^2 i}{\partial t^2}. \qquad \textbf{4.21}$$

Equations **4.20** and **4.21** represent, respectively, voltage and current waves with wave velocity $\sqrt{(1/LC)}$.

Values of L and C for a specimen of ordinary household connecting flex are 7×10^{-7} Hm^{-1} and 6×10^{-11} Fm^{-1} respectively. The wave velocity is therefore $1 \cdot 54 \times 10^8$ ms^{-1}, which is rather more than half the velocity of light in vacuum $(3 \times 10^8$ ms$^{-1})$.

We can calculate the wavelength for 50 Hz alternating current in household flex from the relationship

Wave velocity = frequency × wavelength;

this gives λ to be 3080 km. The length of the lines over which alternating current is transmitted are very much smaller than this, so that the signals are transmitted practically instantaneously compared with the period of the signal; it is therefore unnecessary to speak of waves in this context, but, when the signal frequency is high, the wave nature of the transmission line can become important.

The wave velocity can be decreased by using cable with a higher value for the product LC; a complete analysis of this problem shows that the value of LC is determined solely by the nature of the insulation and is independent of the geometry of the conductors. The time taken for a wave to travel distances of the order of a metre (e.g. about 5×10^{-9} s for coaxial cable) is significant in electronic terms; this is the basis of the so-called delay line.

One example of the use of a delay line is in the trigger mechanism of good-quality cathode-ray oscilloscopes. When randomly occurring pulses are to be displayed, the leading edge of the pulse has to be used to trigger the sweep mechanism; that is, to start the spot off on its journey across the screen. The incoming pulse is split into two; the first part is used to trigger the sweep, whilst the second part is passed along a delay line timed so that its leading edge arrives at the plates immediately after the spot has begun to move. In this way, the whole of the pulse is displayed upon the screen. Delay lines are also used in computers.

In this chapter we have seen how the equation

$$\frac{\partial^2 y}{\partial x^2} = \frac{1}{c^2} \frac{\partial^2 y}{\partial t^2}$$

arises in a variety of physical situations. It is by no means the only wave equation; any partial differential equation relating a displacement in a medium to the spatial coordinates and time is a wave equation. But the above equation is the simplest general description of the essentials of wave motion.

Chapter 5
Further Physical Considerations

5.1 **Introduction**

This chapter is concerned with the general solution of

$$\frac{\partial^2 y}{\partial t^2} = c^2 \frac{\partial^2 y}{\partial x^2} \qquad \textbf{5.1}$$

and the physical implications of the solution. We saw in Chapter 3 how **5.1** is obtained from the wave $y = f(x - ct)$. This means that $y = f(x - ct)$ is a solution of **5.1**; we showed that $y = g(x + ct)$ is also a solution of the equation. (We call the function here g since it need not be the same function as the previous one.) Further, since the original wave equation is a *linear* partial differential equation, *any* linear sum of these two solutions is itself a solution. That is to say, a perfectly good solution of the wave equation **5.1** is

$$y = f(x - ct) + g(x + ct). \qquad \textbf{5.2}$$

In fact, it can be shown (but we shall not do so) that **5.2** is the *general solution* to the wave equation. This is commonly referred to as D'Alembert's solution.

There are two very striking things about this solution. The first is that it gives us a good deal of information about possible waves in a one-dimensional system governed by the wave equation **5.1**. It tells us that either or both directions of wave propagation are possible (a superimposition of waves in both directions being the general case, and special cases of one direction only being when either f or g is zero). Static equilibrium is also consistent with the wave equation, since f and g can both be zero. There is, of course, no wave at all in this trivial case, but it would be strange if the wave equation explicitly ruled out the possibility of the system existing in a state of static equilibrium. Another important fact that **5.2** tells us is that the speed has to be the same for both directions of propagation. As we have seen in the previous chapter, the value of c is determined solely by the physical properties of the wave system under consideration.

The second important feature about the solution **5.2** concerns the *lack* of information it gives. Not only can the waves travel (with equal speed) in either direction, but they can be of any form whatsoever, since there is no effective restriction on the nature of the functions f and g. So it becomes apparent that a waveform of *any* shape may be propagated in accordance with the wave equation. This, after all, ties up with our everyday experience. The air around us will transmit sound waves in accordance with the three-dimensional equivalent of the wave equation **5.1**, and shows absolutely no preference to any particular signal. It will transmit Beethoven, Bartok and Bernstein with equal ease (and, indeed, at the same speed!); this enviable versatility is the prominent feature of D'Alembert's solution.

2 Initial and boundary conditions

Although the solution **5.2** of the wave equation **5.1** is very general, this does not imply that the solution under any circumstances is so general. In this section we shall examine in some detail the factors which restrict the generality of the solution, and to do this we shall take the case of a stretched string.

2.1 *Initial conditions*

Consider a very long stretched string, so long that it can be thought of as being of infinite length. We already know that any transverse wave propagated along the string must have a velocity $\sqrt{(T/\mu)}$ where T and μ are the tension and mass per unit length of the string respectively. We also know, from the previous section, that a wave of any shape may be propagated, subject to certain conditions, the most obvious one being that the shape must be represented by a *continuous* function – any discontinuity would correspond to a break in the string which would certainly not be propagated along its length.

Suppose initially we make the string take a certain shape, which we can describe by the function $\phi(x)$, and suppose that at time $t = 0$ we release the string. A wave will be propagated along the string according to the equation **5.2**. We already know that the general shape of the string at any subsequent time t is given by

$$y = f(x - ct) + g(x + ct).\qquad\qquad\text{[5.2]}$$

We must interpret this equation in the light of our knowledge that at time $t = 0$

$$[y]_{t=0} = \phi(x).\qquad\qquad\textbf{5.3}$$

Equation **5.3** states the initial position of every particle of the string; the left-hand side is merely a convenient shorthand for the value of the function y at time $t = 0$. Since we are constraining the string until time $t = 0$, at which time we are 'letting go', the initial velocities of all particles in the string are zero. That is to say,

$$\left[\frac{\partial y}{\partial t}\right]_{t=0} = 0.\qquad\qquad\textbf{5.4}$$

The two equations **5.3** and **5.4** describe what are known as *initial conditions* which, as we shall now see, restrict the generality of **5.2**. By making t zero in **5.2** we get

$$[y]_{t=0} = f(x) + g(x).$$

But this, from **5.3**, is equal to $\phi(x)$, i.e.

$$f(x) + g(x) = \phi(x). \qquad \qquad \textbf{5.5}$$

Let us now return to **5.2** and differentiate it partially with respect to t:

$$\frac{\partial y}{\partial t} = \frac{\partial}{\partial t} f(x - ct) + \frac{\partial}{\partial t} g(x + ct)$$

$$= \frac{df(x - ct)}{d(x - ct)} \frac{\partial(x - ct)}{\partial t} + \frac{dg(x + ct)}{d(x + ct)} \frac{\partial(x + ct)}{\partial t}$$

$$= -c \frac{df(x - ct)}{d(x - ct)} + c \frac{dg(x + ct)}{d(x + ct)}.$$

At time $t = 0$ this reduces to

$$\left[\frac{\partial y}{\partial t} \right]_{t=0} = -c \frac{df(x)}{dx} + c \frac{dg(x)}{dx}.$$

By cross-multiplying, we see that this becomes

$$\frac{1}{c} \left[\frac{\partial y}{\partial t} \right]_{t=0} dx = -df(x) + dg(x),$$

and by integrating with respect to x we obtain

$$\frac{1}{c} \int \left[\frac{\partial y}{\partial t} \right]_{t=0} dx = -f(x) + g(x). \qquad \qquad \textbf{5.6}$$

If we now subtract **5.6** from **5.5** we obtain

$$2f(x) = \phi(x) - \frac{1}{c} \int \left[\frac{\partial y}{\partial t} \right]_{t=0} dx \qquad \qquad \textbf{5.7}$$

and if we add together **5.5** and **5.6** we obtain

$$2g(x) = \phi(x) + \frac{1}{c} \int \left[\frac{\partial y}{\partial t} \right]_{t=0} dx. \qquad \qquad \textbf{5.8}$$

These last two equations define the general functions f and g of D'Alembert's solution in terms of the initial conditions we have imposed on the problem. In the particular case we are considering, we have assumed that the initial velocities of all particles of the string are zero, as stated in **5.4**. We can immediately see that this effects a considerable simplification in **5.7** and **5.8** by getting rid of both integrals, and the equations become

$$f(x) = \tfrac{1}{2}\phi(x)$$

and $\quad g(x) = \tfrac{1}{2}\phi(x).$

Substituting these back into equation **5.2** we get

$$y = \tfrac{1}{2}\phi(x - ct) + \tfrac{1}{2}\phi(x + ct). \qquad\qquad\qquad \textbf{5.9}$$

To illustrate the meaning of **5.9**, let us consider a particular initial shape $\phi(x)$, illustrated in Figure 24. Here the uniform string, which is under tension T, is

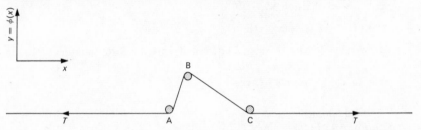

Figure 24 An example of initial conditions in a long string

bent into the shape shown, by three pegs A, B and C. We can imagine the horizontal axis as x and the vertical as $\phi(x)$. The pegs are all removed at the same instant (time $t = 0$). What is the subsequent behaviour of the string? First of all, **5.9** very properly tells us that, at time $t = 0$, y is indeed equal to $\phi(x)$, the two terms on the right-hand side each contributing half. But at a later time the two halves will not be, as they were at the beginning, coincident in space. In fact the first term in **5.9** represents the initial shape (scaled down by a factor of two) travelling to the right with speed c, while the second term represents the

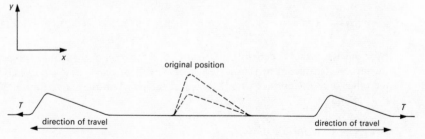

Figure 25 Appearance of the string of Figure 24 at a later time

same shape (similarly scaled down) travelling to the left with the same speed. At a subsequent time, therefore, the string would look as in Figure 25.

As time goes on, the two disturbances in the string proceed away from each other at a constant relative velocity $2c$.

5.2.2 *Stationary waves*

Arising from the subject of initial conditions is a very important special case. Let us suppose that the initial shape of the string is cosinusoidal (i.e. the shape of a cosine curve) throughout its length, with wavelength λ. That is to say,

$$\phi(x) = a \cos 2\pi \frac{x}{\lambda}.$$

5.10

As before, the initial velocities of all the particles comprising the string are zero and so equation **5.9**,

$$y = \tfrac{1}{2}\phi(x - ct) + \tfrac{1}{2}\phi(x + ct),$$

is again valid. When we insert the form of ϕ given in **5.10**, equation **5.9** becomes

$$y = \tfrac{1}{2}a \cos \frac{2\pi}{\lambda}(x - ct) + \tfrac{1}{2}a \cos \frac{2\pi}{\lambda}(x + ct).$$

5.11

This equation describes the subsequent motion of the string. Now, we can rewrite **5.11** in the form

$$y = a \cos \frac{1}{2}\left[\frac{4\pi x}{\lambda}\right] \cos \frac{1}{2}\left[-\frac{4\pi ct}{\lambda}\right].$$

[The trigonometrical identity

$$\cos A + \cos B = 2 \cos \tfrac{1}{2}(A + B) \cos \tfrac{1}{2}(A - B)$$

has been used, and we can ignore the minus sign in the argument of the second cosine term since $\cos \theta = \cos(-\theta)$.] We can replace λ/c in this term by τ, the period. So the last equation simplifies to

$$y = a \cos \frac{2\pi x}{\lambda} \cos \frac{2\pi t}{\tau}.$$

5.12

Now this is a rather peculiar result. Instead of a function of the $f(x \pm ct)$ type, we have the product of two cosine terms, one involving only x as a variable and the other only t. Consider what happens at the point on the string for which $x = 0$. Since

$$\cos \frac{2\pi x}{\lambda} = 1 \qquad \text{for } x = 0,$$

equation **5.12** becomes

$$[y]_{x=0} = a \cos \frac{2\pi t}{\tau}.$$

So the particle at $x = 0$ just bobs up and down, executing simple harmonic motion with period τ. Consider another particle, say one eighth of a wavelength away from $x = 0$. Here

$$x = \frac{\lambda}{8}.$$

Thus $\dfrac{x}{\lambda} = \dfrac{1}{8}$

and **5.12** gives us

$$[y]_{x=\frac{1}{8}\lambda} = a \cos \frac{\pi}{4} \cos \frac{2\pi t}{\tau} = \frac{a}{\sqrt 2} \cos \frac{2\pi t}{\tau}.$$

At this point along the string, therefore, the particle is executing simple harmonic motion with the same period but with reduced amplitude.

Let us proceed further and consider what happens at a point a quarter wavelength to the right of $x = 0$. This is the point $x = \frac{1}{4}\lambda$ or $x/\lambda = \frac{1}{4}$. Equation **5.12** now becomes

$$[y]_{x=\frac{1}{4}\lambda} = a \cos \frac{\pi}{2} \cos \frac{2\pi t}{\tau} = 0,$$

since $\cos \dfrac{\pi}{2} = 0.$

Therefore this point *does not move at any time*. In fact there is a series of such points, namely those for which

$$\cos \frac{2\pi x}{\lambda} = 0,$$

or $\quad \dfrac{2\pi x}{\lambda} = \pm \dfrac{\pi}{2}, \pm \dfrac{3\pi}{2}, \pm \dfrac{5\pi}{2}, \ldots,$

i.e. $\quad \dfrac{2\pi x}{\lambda} = (2n + 1)\dfrac{\pi}{2} \qquad (n = \ldots, -2, -1, 0, 1, 2, \ldots),$

i.e. $\quad x = (2n + 1)\dfrac{\lambda}{4}.$

These points of no displacement are called *nodes*. Since any two adjacent nodes are a distance $\frac{1}{2}\lambda$ apart, half-way between the nth and $(n + 1)$th nodes the value of x will be given by

$$
\begin{aligned}
x &= (2n + 1)\tfrac{1}{4}\lambda + \tfrac{1}{4}\lambda \\
&= (2n + 2)\tfrac{1}{4}\lambda \\
&= (n + 1)\tfrac{1}{2}\lambda.
\end{aligned}
$$

For this value of x,

$$
\cos \frac{2\pi x}{\lambda} = \cos \left\{ 2\pi(n + 1)\frac{\lambda}{2\lambda} \right\}
$$

$$
= \cos[(n + 1)\pi] = \pm 1.
$$

Such points will therefore oscillate in accordance with the equation

$$
y = \pm a \cos \frac{2\pi t}{\tau}.
$$

No point can have a greater amplitude than this (since unity is the maximum value of the cosine function). Thus, half-way between each adjacent pair of nodes we have a point of maximum vibration. These points are known as *antinodes*.

Figure 26 shows the profile of the string at different times. It is seen that there is apparently no wave travelling along the x-axis in either direction, the two constituent travelling waves in this case adding up to give a stationary effect. Such a superposition is called a *standing wave* or *stationary wave*, and is of great importance, as we shall see later.

We must stress an important mathematical feature of standing waves. We saw that the standing waves in this particular case are described by equation **5.12**, i.e.

$$
y = a \cos \frac{2\pi x}{\lambda} \cos \frac{2\pi t}{\tau}.
$$

This is no longer of the form

$$
y = f(x \pm ct)
$$

but is, rather, the *product* of two functions, $\cos(2\pi x/\lambda)$, which is a function of the position x only, and $\cos(2\pi t/\tau)$, which is a function of the time t only. Standing waves are always described in this way, and, in general, we can write

$$
y = X(x)\,T(t),
$$

where $X(x)$ and $T(t)$ are, respectively, functions of position and time only. Whenever we see a wave represented by an equation of this type, we know at once that a standing wave is indicated. It is doubtful whether this situation is, indeed, correctly describable as wave motion since there is no net flow of energy in any direction.

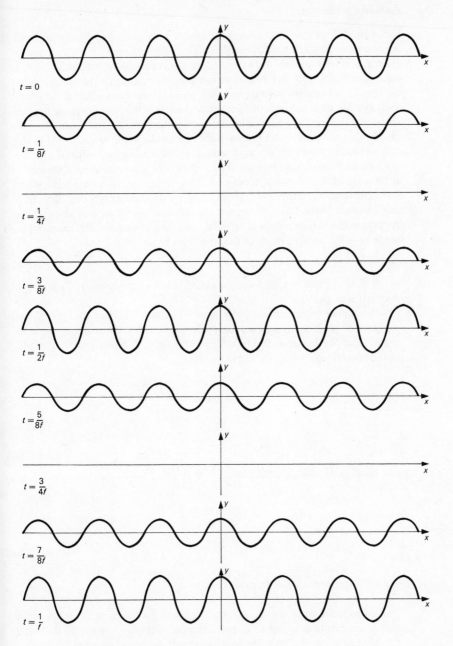

Figure 26 Standing-wave patterns at different times

5.2.3 Boundary conditions

Initial conditions specify the displacement, or rate of change of displacement, or some other characteristic of every particle of the system at a particular instant of time, and we have seen that they reduce the generality of the solution of the wave equation **5.1**. In this section we are going to investigate the effect of what are known as *boundary conditions*, which occur in problems where we impose a restriction on what happens to a *particular* particle in the system as time goes on. These two different types of conditions are rather similar; in the one case we specify what happens at all values of x for a particular value of t, and in the other case we specify what happens at all values of t for a particular value of x.

To illustrate the ideas involved in boundary conditions, let us refer once more to the case of the uniform, tensioned string. Suppose we have such a string stretching from $x = 0$ to $x = \infty$. At the point $x = 0$ the string is firmly clamped so that it cannot move. Since the transverse displacement of a point at distance x from the origin at time t is $y(x, t)$, as before, the restriction placed by the clamping on the possible wave motions of the string can be stated as

$$y(0, t) = 0 \qquad\qquad\qquad\qquad\textbf{5.13}$$

for all time t. Equation **5.13** is a *boundary condition* that we are imposing in this particular problem.

Now suppose we are able to propagate a transverse wave of the form shown in Figure 27, and described by a function $f(x, t)$, along the string towards the origin. Since the disturbance is travelling in the negative direction of x, the wave must be described by $y = f(x + ct)$.

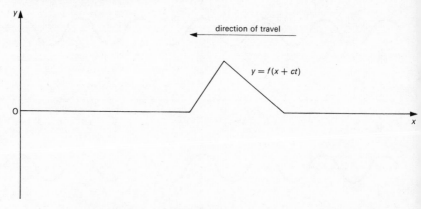

Figure 27 Transverse wave on a clamped string

What happens when the disturbance arrives at the clamp at $x = 0$? A simple experiment can help us here. A length of cord (a clothes line would do nicely) is firmly tied at one end to some fixed object and the other end is held fairly taut.

If the held end is now given a sudden single flick, it is seen that the resulting disturbance travels down the cord to the tied end where it turns round and retraces its path back towards the hand-held end of the string.

What can we tell about this return wave? Firstly it must travel with same speed as the outward-going wave since, as we have seen, the speed is determined entirely by the tension and mass per unit length of the string. We shall make no assumptions about the shape of the return wave, and shall describe it by the function

$$y = g(x - ct).$$

As the incident wave reaches the point of clamping at $x = 0$ it can cause no transverse motion of the string, because the string is not free to move. It follows, therefore, that the return wave is one of such a shape as to cancel out the lateral displacement of the incident wave at $x = 0$. In other words, the displacement of the incident wave is exactly equal and opposite to the displacement due to the return wave at all times, so that when we add the two displacements together at $x = 0$ the result is always zero.

This is an example of the very important *principle of superposition*, which tells us that if waves are superposed the net displacement is the sum of the displacements due to each of the waves acting independently of the others. D'Alembert's solution

$$y = f(x - ct) + g(x + ct) \qquad\qquad [5.2]$$

is an example of the principle of superposition.

The diagrams in Figure 28 show the incident wave at various stages after the arrival at the clamped point $x = 0$. With the knowledge that the return wave has to be of such shape as to cancel the displacement at $x = 0$ due to the incident wave, we can build up the shape of the return wave as shown, bearing in mind that both waves have the same speed. Since the displacement due to the incident wave is upwards, the displacement due to the return wave must be downward. If we follow the sequences in Figure 28 through, we see that the shape of the wave has also been reversed in the x-direction. In other words, the original wave has been turned back-to-front and upside down.

Mathematically, we can represent the process as follows. When we insert the boundary condition 5.13 into 5.2 for $x = 0$, we obtain

$$[y]_{x=0} = f(ct) + g(-ct) = 0.$$
Thus $\quad f(ct) = -g(-ct),$

so we find that the relationship between the functions f and g for this case is

$$f(ct - x) = -g(x - ct).$$

Thus, from equation 5.2,

$$y = f(x + ct) - f(ct - x). \qquad\qquad \textbf{5.14}$$

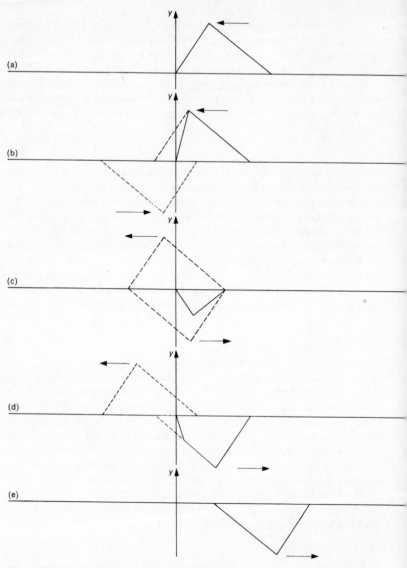

Figure 28 Wave reflection in a clamped string

The implication of equation **5.14** is that if we propagate a wave described by the function $f(x + ct)$ down the string, a second wave represented by $-f(ct - x)$ develops because of the restriction imposed at the origin. How is this latter function related to the original one? To understand this, we note that $f(x - ct)$

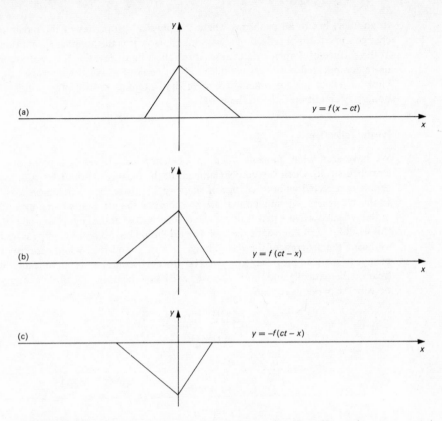

Figure 29 Illustration of the relationship between the functions $f(x-ct)$, $f(ct-x)$ and $-f(ct-x)$

would be of exactly the same shape as $f(x+ct)$ but travelling in the opposite direction. It can also be noticed that $f(ct-x)$ is the same as $f(-\{x-ct\})$, so we are faced with the question of the relationship of $f(X)$ to $f(-X)$. A little thought will enable one to see that these functions are mirror images of one another, the line of reflection being the y-axis (Figure 29b). Finally we note that there is a minus sign in front of $f(ct-x)$. This, of course, implies an additional reflection of the function about the x-axis (Figure 29c).

Let us now summarize the consequences of the imposition of this boundary condition. The original wave incident on the boundary (namely $f(x+ct)$) is reflected back with an equal velocity from the origin. Moreover the reflected wave is of the same shape as the incident wave, except that the shape is reversed left-to-right and has been turned upside down. This reflection process is very common in nature and, although we have taken as an example a particularly simple boundary condition, a great variety of such conditions have just this effect, that of producing a reflected wave. The details vary from one situation to another, but in all problems where the physical properties of the medium change some form of reflection always takes place. It is the boundary condition at the surface of a mirror that causes it to reflect light waves, and it is a rather more complicated boundary condition at the bank of a river which causes the bank to reflect surface water waves. We shall examine several other kinds of boundary conditions later in the book.

5.3   Partial reflection

We have seen what happens when an incident wave arrives at a point on a stretched string which is securely clamped. In the ideal situation described, the profile is reflected without change of shape (apart from the inversion process). In this treatment, we implied that all the energy in the incident wave appeared in the reflected wave – that is, there was no energy loss at the clamp. In practice, this would not, of course, be the case. Energy would be lost at the clamp (as well as during the progress of the wave along the string) and this would result in a change of shape in the reflected wave. The process becomes quite complicated to treat mathematically and this is why we have made the rather idealized assumptions in the previous section.

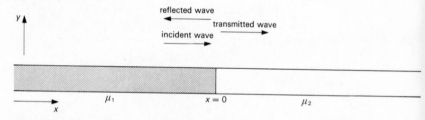

Figure 30 The junction of two stretched elastic strings. The arrows indicate the direction of travel of the transverse waves

We will now go on to see what happens when the physical characteristics of the string change at some point. Suppose, for example, we have two stretched strings, both very long but of different mass per unit length, joined together as shown in Figure 30. Let the join be at the point $x = 0$ and let the left- and right-hand strings have masses per unit length μ_1 and μ_2 respectively. Let us assume that a harmonic wave is sent along the left-hand string in the direction from left to right. We will use the exponential representation for harmonic waves which we discussed in Chapter 3.

Let the incident wave be

$$y_i = A_i \exp 2\pi i(f_i t - k_i x).$$ 5.15

Here, the suffix i indicates the incident wave, A_i is the amplitude (a real number); f_i and k_i are, respectively, the frequency and the wave number of the wave.

What happens when this wave arrives at the junction at $x = 0$? Let us assume that part of the disturbance is transmitted into the second string, but that the other part is reflected back along the left-hand string. This is not begging the question as might at first appear. If, in fact, there is no wave reflected or no wave transmitted, our analysis will show this. We may, therefore, represent the transmitted and reflected waves quite generally as follows

$$y_t = A_t \exp 2\pi i(f_t t - k_t x), \qquad\qquad\qquad\qquad\qquad \textbf{5.16}$$

$$y_r = A_r \exp 2\pi i(f_r t + k_r x), \qquad\qquad\qquad\qquad\qquad \textbf{5.17}$$

where the suffixes t and r refer to the transmitted and reflected wave respectively (see Figure 30). If it turns out that there are phase changes at the junction, A_t and A_r will prove to be complex quantities (or negative if the phase change is π).

Now by the principle of superposition, the total disturbance in the left-hand string will be the superposition of the incident and reflected waves. We can write this as

$$y_1 = y_i + y_r.$$

The total disturbance in the right-hand string is just the transmitted wave, so

$$y_2 = y_t.$$

Let us now examine the physical conditions which govern the values of y_1 and y_2 at the junction. Firstly, if the string does not come apart, the values of y_1 and y_2 must always be the same, so

$$(y_1)_{x=0} = (y_2)_{x=0}$$

or $\quad [y_i + y_r]_{x=0} = [y_t]_{x=0}.$ $\qquad\qquad\qquad\qquad\qquad\qquad$ **5.18**

The second condition is not so obvious. We saw in Chapter 4 that the transverse force acting at a point on a stretched string under tension T along which waves are travelling, is $T \, \partial y/\partial x$. Now this force must be the same on both sides of the junction. Suppose for a moment that the transverse forces are different at the ends of the two parts of the string at the junction. This would mean that the force would change by a finite amount across the boundary. Now, ideally, the boundary has no extent or size at all, it is an abrupt change from one string to the other, corresponding to a geometrical point. So if the transverse forces were different, we should have a finite net force (i.e. the difference between the forces on either side) acting upon a vanishingly small object. This, according to Newton's second law of motion, would lead to infinite acceleration of the junction (since the strings have finite mass per unit length), so we conclude that transverse forces on both sides of the junction must be the same. Thus

$$T \left(\frac{\partial y_1}{\partial x} \right)_{x=0} = T \left(\frac{\partial y_2}{\partial x} \right)_{x=0}. \qquad\qquad\qquad\qquad \textbf{5.19}$$

Let us substitute the expressions for y_i, y_t and y_r (equations **5.15**, **5.16** and **5.17**) into **5.18**, putting $x = 0$. We get

$$A_i \exp 2\pi i f_i\, t + A_r \exp 2\pi i f_r\, t = A_t \exp 2\pi i f_t\, t. \qquad \textbf{5.20}$$

If we differentiate **5.15** with respect to x we get

$$\frac{\partial y_i}{\partial x} = -2\pi i k_1 A_i \exp 2\pi i (f_i\, t - k_1 x),$$

with almost identical expressions for $\partial y_t/\partial x$ and $\partial y_r/\partial x$; if we now substitute these into **5.19**, putting $x = 0$, we get

$$-iA_i k_i \exp 2\pi i f_i\, t + iA_r k_r \exp 2\pi i f_r\, t = -iA_t k_t \exp 2\pi i f_t\, t. \qquad \textbf{5.21}$$

Now equation **5.20** involves real and imaginary quantities, and it has to hold for all values of the time t. This can only happen if the exponential terms cancel out, which means that

$$f_i = f_r = f_t.$$

This is a result that could be predicted physically, for it is clearly impossible for the frequency of the transmitted wave to be different from that of the incident wave, whilst f_i and f_r must be the same since they are determined by T and μ_1 only. We can now replace f_i, f_r and f_t by the single quantity f.

With this substitution, **5.20** becomes

$$A_i + A_r = A_t \qquad \textbf{5.22}$$

and **5.21** becomes

$$A_i k_i - A_r k_r = A_t k_t. \qquad \textbf{5.23}$$

Now we have seen that

$$c = \sqrt{\frac{T}{\mu}} = f\lambda = \frac{f}{k}.$$

Therefore $k_i = k_r$;

also $k_i = f\sqrt{\left(\dfrac{\mu_1}{T}\right)}$ and $k_t = f\sqrt{\left(\dfrac{\mu_2}{T}\right)}$, $\qquad \textbf{5.24}$

that is, the incident and reflected waves have the same wave number.

We can rewrite **5.23** as

$$A_i k_r - A_r k_i = A_t k_t. \qquad \textbf{5.25}$$

Solving the simultaneous equations **5.22** and **5.25** for A_t and A_r, we get

$$A_t = A_i \frac{2k_i}{k_i + k_t}, \qquad \textbf{5.26}$$

$$A_r = A_i \frac{k_i - k_t}{k_i + k_t} \cdot$$

We now know the amplitudes of the reflected and transmitted waves in terms of the amplitude of the incident wave. Further, since the quantities on the right-hand sides of **5.26** and **5.27** are all real, A_t and A_r are both real numbers and there is no phase change involved, *except* when $k_t > k_i$ whereupon A_r has the opposite sign to A_i, indicating that the reflected wave has undergone a phase-change of π radians with respect to the incident wave.

Now we can introduce the tension and masses per unit length of the two parts of the string from equation **5.24**.

When we do this we get

$$A_t = \frac{A_i \, 2\sqrt{\mu_1}}{\sqrt{\mu_1} + \sqrt{\mu_2}}$$

and $\quad A_r = A_i \dfrac{\sqrt{\mu_1} - \sqrt{\mu_2}}{\sqrt{\mu_1} + \sqrt{\mu_2}},$

so the change of phase on reflection occurs only when $\mu_2 > \mu_1$, that is, when the mass per unit length of the string on the right is greater than that on the left.

4 **Energy in a travelling wave**

Finally in this chapter on solutions to the non-dispersive wave equation (see 1.2.2) we will consider briefly the propagation of energy in a wave, taking transverse waves on a string as our example.

In the absence of a wave, the kinetic energy is zero since no particle in the string has any velocity, and, since we can choose the zero of potential energy arbitrarily, we will assume that the potential energy is also zero. When a travelling wave of transverse displacement $y(x,t)$ is being propagated along the string, the latter is stretched locally, thus acquiring potential energy. Figure 31 shows an infinitesimal length of the string, from which we see that a section of the string, which in the absence of a wave is of length dx, has now a length ds. The section has thus been stretched by an amount $ds - dx$. The constant force exerted during this stretching is T, the tension in the string, and thus the potential energy dE_P acquired by the length is

$$dE_P = T(ds - dx),$$

which, by reference to Figure 31, becomes

$$dE_P = T[(dx^2 + dy^2)^{1/2} - dx]$$

$$= T \, dx \left[\left\{ 1 + \left(\frac{\partial y}{\partial x} \right)^2 \right\}^{1/2} - 1 \right] \cdot$$

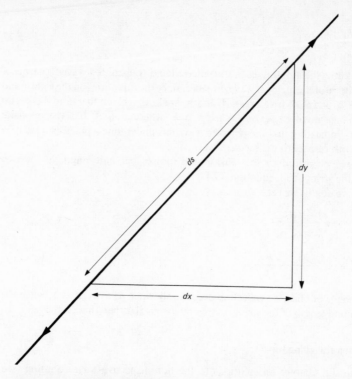

Figure 31 A section of stretched string while a transverse wave (upward displacement) is being propagated horizontally, showing the relationship between *ds*, *dy* and *dx*

By the binomial theorem this finally becomes

$$dE_{\mathrm{P}} = \tfrac{1}{2}T\left(\frac{\partial y}{\partial x}\right)^2 dx.$$

5.28

The kinetic energy dE_{K} of the element is

$$dE_{\mathrm{K}} = \tfrac{1}{2}\,(\text{mass of element}) \times (\text{velocity of element})^2$$

$$= \tfrac{1}{2}\mu\,dx\left(\frac{\partial y}{\partial t}\right)^2.$$

5.29

If we denote the total energy of the element by dE, we see from **5.28** and **5.29** that

$$dE = \frac{dx}{2} \left[\mu \left(\frac{\partial y}{\partial t} \right)^2 + T \left(\frac{\partial y}{\partial x} \right)^2 \right].$$

We now define the *energy density*, $D(x,t)$ as the energy per unit length. Thus

$$D(x,t) = \frac{1}{2} \left[\mu \left(\frac{\partial y}{\partial t} \right)^2 + T \left(\frac{\partial y}{\partial x} \right)^2 \right]. \qquad \textbf{5.30}$$

Let us calculate D for the harmonic wave represented by

$$y = A \cos 2\pi(kx - ft). \qquad \textbf{5.31}$$

If we differentiate **5.31** partially and substitute into **5.30** we obtain

$$D(x,t) = \frac{4\pi^2}{2} A^2 \sin^2 2\pi(kx - ft) [\mu f^2 + Tk^2].$$

We now take μ outside the square bracket and obtain

$$D(x,t) = \frac{4\pi^2}{2} \mu A^2 \sin^2 2\pi(kx - ft) \left[f^2 + \frac{T}{\mu} k^2 \right].$$

Since $T/\mu = c^2$ the contents of the square bracket become $[f^2 + c^2k^2]$, which, since $f^2 = c^2k^2$ finally becomes $2f^2$. Thus

$$D(x,t) = 4\pi^2 \mu A^2 f^2 \sin^2 2\pi(kx - ft). \qquad \textbf{5.32}$$

So we see that the energy in the wave is propagated as the function of $(kx - ft)$ described in the right-hand side of **5.32**; it is thus propagated with the speed $f/k = c$ of the displacement wave.

Actually, the frequency f and wave number k of the displacement wave are not those of the energy-density wave. Since

$$\sin^2 \theta = \tfrac{1}{2}(1 - \cos 2\theta),$$

it follows that

$$D(x,t) = 2\pi^2 \mu A^2 f^2 [1 - \cos 2\pi(2kx - 2ft)]. \qquad \textbf{5.33}$$

Thus the energy-density wave propagates with a frequency twice that of the displacement wave and a wavelength of half that of the displacement wave, but, as mentioned above, the *velocity* is the same as that of the displacement wave. The spatial part of the energy-density and displacement waves are shown in Figure 32.

The energy in length dx is $D(x,t)\,dx$, and therefore the energy in one wavelength is

$$\int_0^\lambda D(x,t)\,dx,$$

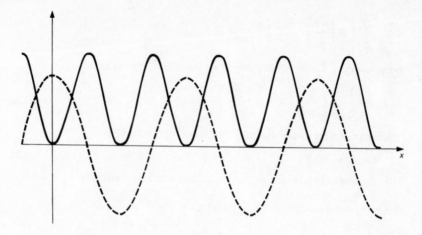

Figure 32 The dotted line represents the profile of the displacement wave **5.31**, and the solid line the corresponding energy-density wave **5.33** for time $t = 0$. The scales of the ordinates are arbitrary

which, from **5.33**, becomes

$$\int_0^\lambda 2\pi^2 \mu A^2 f^2 [1 - \cos 2\pi(2kx - 2ft)]\,dx.$$

The integral of the cosine term is zero; and the energy contained in a wavelength is thus

$$\int_0^\lambda 2\pi^2 \mu A^2 f^2\,dx = 2\pi^2 \mu A^2 f^2 \lambda.$$

Now this energy takes a time τ to pass a given point. Therefore the energy flowing per unit time (the power P) is given by

$$P = \frac{2\pi^2 \mu A^2 f^2 \lambda}{\tau}$$

$$= 2\pi^2 \mu A^2 f^2 c.$$

We see, therefore, that the power transmitted by the wave is proportional to the square of the amplitude and the square of the frequency. A similar result obtains for many other types of harmonic wave, including sound waves. That light intensity is proportional to the square of the amplitude of the disturbance is an analogous result which will be used in Chapter 9.

Chapter 6
Fourier's Theorem

Introduction and mathematical discussion

The theorem of J. B. J. Fourier, in various guises, ranks among the most important propositions in physics. It is probably true to say that there is no important branch of the subject which this theorem has not illuminated in some way or other. Although it finds its main use in studies involving wave motion, Fourier first introduced it, in 1822, in connection with the problem of heat conduction, in which subject it still occupies an important position. These two applications themselves illustrate the diversity of situations to which it has been applied.

Fourier's theorem is essentially a trigonometrical relationship which can be applied to a large class of mathematical functions, of which periodic functions provide the simplest examples. We will deal with periodic functions first, and later on in this chapter go on to non-periodic functions.

Mathematically, a periodic function of time $g(t)$, of period τ, is a function which has the property that

$$g(t + \tau) = g(t),$$

for all values of t. By a simple iteration of this expression one can see that

$$g(t + N\tau) = g(t),$$

for all t, where N is any integer, positive, negative or zero. It necessarily follows that the function extends infinitely along the positive and negative t-axes.

Figure 33 illustrates some periodic functions, each of the same period τ; in particular, Figure 33(a) illustrates the function

$$y(t) = A \cos\left(\frac{2\pi t}{\tau} + \phi\right)$$

plotted against time. The profile of this is sinusoidal, the amplitude is A and the phase angle ϕ determines how far the first maximum is away from the origin. If we substitute f_0 for $1/\tau$, the equation becomes

$$y(t) = A \cos(2\pi f_0 t + \phi) \tag{6.1}$$

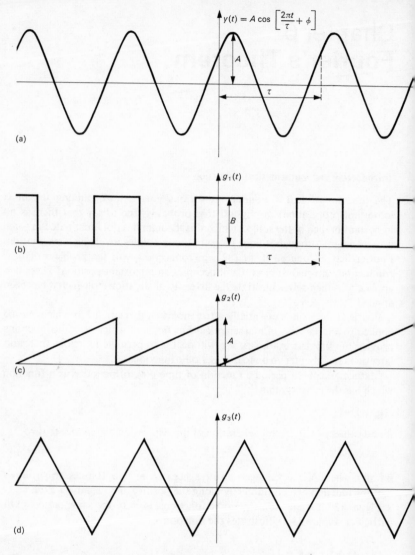

$$y(t) = A \cos \left[\frac{2\pi t}{\tau} + \phi \right]$$

(a)

$g_1(t)$

(b)

$g_2(t)$

(c)

$g_3(t)$

(d)

Figure 33 Some periodic functions of time

Now Fourier's theorem states that *any* periodic function $g(t)$ can be expressed as the sum (to an infinite number of terms if necessary) of functions of the type appearing in equation **6.1**, where the frequencies appropriate to each term in the sum are integral multiples, nf_0 of f_0, and the amplitudes A and phases ϕ are, in general, different for different values of n. The theorem implies that any periodic function of time can be *analysed* into *frequency components*; alternatively the

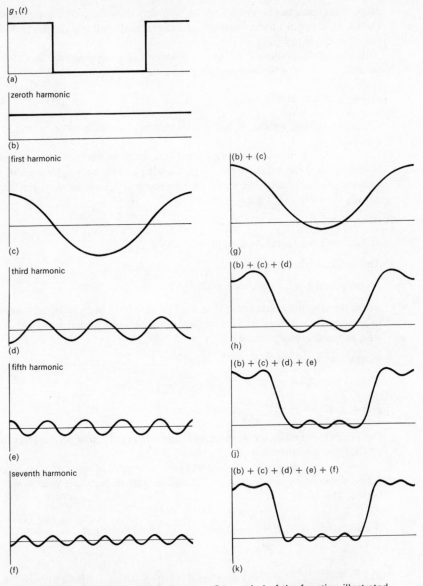

Figure 34 Illustration of Fourier's theorem. One period of the function illustrated in Figure 33(b) appears in (a). The curves (b)–(f) on the left-hand side show the first five frequency components into which (a) is analysed. On the right-hand side, (g)–(k) are shown successive stages in the addition of the components in the synthesis of the original function. The last curve (k) is seen to be a reasonable approximation to (a) after the addition of only five terms

original function can be *synthesized* by summing these frequency components. Figure 34 illustrates these processes of analysis and synthesis for the periodic function shown in Figure 33(b).

Expressed in mathematical terms, Fourier's Theorem asserts that, for a periodic function of fundamental frequency f_0,

$$g(t) = \sum_{n=0}^{\infty} A_n \cos(2\pi n f_0 t + \phi_n),$$
6.2

where the suffixes on the As and the ϕs denote that these latter belong to a particular n.

If we wish to Fourier-analyse a given periodic function, our problem essentially is to determine the values of the amplitudes A_n, and phases ϕ_n, for each of its frequency components. We begin by expressing a typical term of the sum, namely

$$A_n \cos(2\pi n f_0 t + \phi_n),$$

as $A_n \cos(2\pi n f_0 t)\cos\phi_n - A_n \sin(2\pi n f_0 t)\sin\phi_n$.

This can be slightly rearranged to

$$(A_n \cos \phi_n)\cos 2\pi n f_0 t - (A_n \sin \phi_n)\sin 2\pi n f_0 t,$$

where those terms which are independent of time have been collected together in brackets. For convenience we can replace these terms respectively by C_n and $-S_n$, so the expression becomes

$$C_n \cos 2\pi n f_0 t + S_n \sin 2\pi n f_0 t.$$

Thus, from **6.2**,

$$g(t) = \sum_{n=0}^{\infty} C_n \cos 2\pi n f_0 t + \sum_{n=0}^{\infty} S_n \sin 2\pi n f_0 t.$$
6.3

Our problem of finding the A_n and ϕ_n appropriate to a particular periodic function $g(t)$ has now become that of finding the C_n and S_n.

Now, concentrating our attention on a particular value of n, say m, we multiply **6.3** throughout by $\cos 2\pi m f_0 t$ and integrate with respect to t over a whole period, obtaining

$$\int_0^{1/f_0} \cos(2\pi m f_0 t)g(t) \, dt = \int_0^{1/f_0} \cos(2\pi m f_0 t)\left(\sum_{n=0}^{\infty} C_n \cos 2\pi n f_0 t \right) dt$$

$$+ \int_0^{1/f_0} \cos(2\pi m f_0 t)\left(\sum_{n=0}^{\infty} S_n \sin 2\pi n f_0 t \right) dt$$
6.4

where the range of the integral (from 0 to τ) has been expressed in terms of f_0. Equation **6.4** appears very long and cumbersome, but we shall now see that remarkable simplifications can be effected on the right-hand side. A typical term in the first integral on the right-hand side is

$$C_n \int_0^{1/f_0} \cos(2\pi m f_0 t) \cos 2\pi n f_0 t \, dt \qquad\qquad \textbf{6.5}$$

and similarly a typical term in the second integral is

$$S_n \int_0^{1/f_0} \cos(2\pi m f_0 t) \sin 2\pi n f_0 t \, dt, \qquad\qquad \textbf{6.6}$$

the quantities C_n and S_n being brought outside the integral sign because they are constants. Let us take **6.5** first, and suppose $m \neq n$. A little thought will reveal that the value of the integral is zero. Figure 35 illustrates this for the case $m = 4$ and $n = 3$, where the first two graphs are those of the two individual cosine terms and the third graph is that of their product. Half the area of the third graph has been shaded with four different shadings; it will be noticed that each type of shading occurs twice, once for a positive area (above the time axis) and once for an equal negative area (below the axis). All the positive areas therefore have equal negative counterparts, producing a zero overall value.

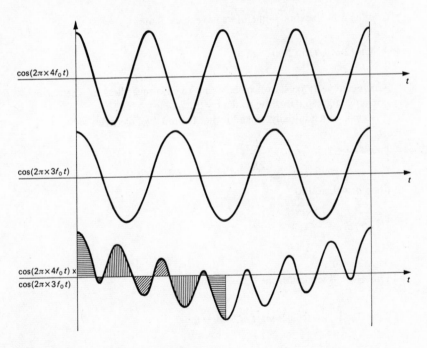

Figure 35 An illustration showing that

$$\int_0^{1/f_0} \cos(2\pi \times 3f_0 t)\cos(2\pi \times 4f_0 t) \, dt = 0$$

Continuing with our consideration of the expression **6.5**, and taking the case where $n = m$, we see that the expression now becomes

$$C_m \int_0^{1/f_0} \cos^2 2\pi m f_0 t \, dt$$

which can easily be shown to be equal to

$$\frac{1}{2f_0} C_m,$$

provided m is not zero. If m is zero, then the expression becomes

$$C_0 \int_0^{1/f_0} dt,$$

which is $\dfrac{1}{f_0} C_0$.

Coming now to expression **6.6**, we have to evaluate

$$\int_0^{1/f_0} \cos(2\pi m f_0 t)\sin 2\pi n f_0 t \, dt,$$

which can easily be shown to be equal to zero regardless of whether $m = n$ or not. (It is suggested that the reader try this.)

So **6.4**, which initially looked rather formidable, has been reduced to

$$\int_0^{1/f_0} g(t)\cos(2\pi m f_0 t) \, dt = \frac{1}{2f_0} C_m$$

when $m \neq 0$, and to

$$\int_0^{1/f_0} g(t) \, dt = \frac{1}{f_0} C_0$$

when $m = 0$.

This gives us values for the C_m as follows:

$$C_m = 2f_0 \int_0^{1/f_0} g(t)\cos 2\pi m f_0 t \, dt, \quad m \neq 0,$$

$$C_0 = f_0 \int_0^{1/f_0} g(t) \, dt.$$

6.7

If we had started from **6.3** by multiplying by $\sin 2\pi m f_0 t$ instead of $\cos 2\pi m f_0 t$, we would, by a precisely similar argument, have arrived at the conclusion that

$$S_m = 2f_0 \int_0^{1/f_0} g(t) \sin 2\pi m f_0 t \, dt. \qquad \textbf{6.8}$$

(So, unlike C_0, S_0 is always zero, since the integral vanishes for $m = 0$.) Equations **6.7** and **6.8** tell us how to find the coefficients C_n and S_n corresponding to a given periodic function $g(t)$, and hence enable us to perform the frequency analysis of any such function.

Let us take as a concrete example the function illustrated in Figure 33(b). Here we have a periodic function $g(t)$, with period τ, whose value is B for times t lying between 0 and $\frac{1}{4}\tau$, and also between $\frac{3}{4}\tau$ and τ, and zero for times between $\frac{1}{4}\tau$ and $\frac{3}{4}\tau$. Equation **6.7** (for $m \neq 0$) becomes

$$C_m = 2f_0 \int_0^{1/4 f_0} B \cos 2\pi m f_0 t \, dt + 2f_0 \int_{3/4 f_0}^{1/f_0} B \cos 2\pi m f_0 t \, dt.$$

Although these integrals can easily be evaluated, a simplification can in this case be effected by noticing that the limits of the second integral can be altered to $-1/4f_0$ and zero, respectively, because the latter time range corresponds to an identical situation as far as the integrand is concerned. Since the second integral now has its upper limit (at $t = 0$) coinciding with the lower limit of the first integral, the two integrals can be combined to give

$$C_m = 2f_0 \int_{-1/4 f_0}^{+1/4 f_0} B \cos 2\pi m f_0 t \, dt$$

$$= 2f_0 B \left[\frac{\sin 2\pi m f_0 t}{2\pi m f_0} \right]_{-1/4 f_0}^{+1/4 f_0}$$

$$= \frac{2B}{m\pi} \sin \tfrac{1}{2} m\pi.$$

If we substitute $m = 1, 2, 3, \ldots$ into this last result, the C_m finally emerge as

$$C_1 = \frac{2B}{\pi}, \qquad C_2 = 0,$$

$$C_3 = \frac{-2}{3\pi} B, \qquad C_4 = 0,$$

$$C_5 = \frac{2}{5\pi} B, \qquad C_6 = 0,$$

$$C_7 = \frac{-2}{7\pi} B, \qquad C_8 = 0, \qquad \text{etc.}$$

From the second of equations **6.7**, C_0 is seen to be $\frac{1}{2}B$.

Having now found the C_m, let us turn our attention to finding the S_m, from **6.8**. With the same limits of integration as before, **6.8** gives

$$S_m = 2f_0 \int_{-1/4f_0}^{+1/4f_0} B \sin 2\pi m f_0 t \, dt$$

$$= -2f_0 B \left[\frac{\cos 2\pi m f_0 t}{2\pi m f_0} \right]_{-1/4f_0}^{+1/4f_0}$$

$$= 0 \qquad \text{for all } m.$$

Thus all the S_m are zero in this case. In fact this is so for *any* periodic function which is also *even* – that is to say, any function $g(t)$ where

$$g(-t) = g(t).$$

The function we have taken, illustrated in Figure 33(b), is clearly even. In a

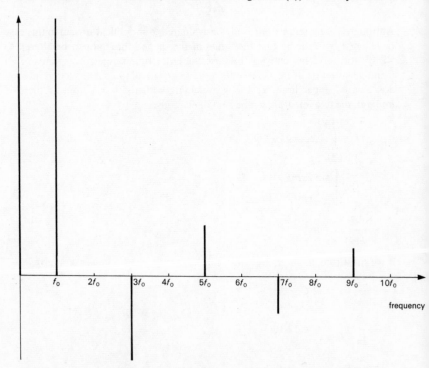

Figure 36 Frequency spectrum of the 'battlement' function g_1, illustrated in Figure 33(b)

similar way, any odd function, i.e. any function for which

$$g(t) = -g(-t)$$

produces zero C_m. Figure 33(d) illustrates such a function.

The C_m for the 'battlement' function [Figure (33b)] can now be displayed in graphical form by vertical lines plotted along an abscissa representing frequency, whose heights are proportional to the C_m. The result is shown in Figure 36. This is the *frequency spectrum* of the original function $g_1(t)$. The frequency f_0 $(=1/\tau)$ is termed the *fundamental frequency* or, alternatively, the *first harmonic*. The frequency $2f_0$ is termed the *first overtone* or *second harmonic*, $3f_0$ is the *second overtone* or *third harmonic* and so on. For the $g_1(t)$ we have chosen, the even harmonics are said to be 'missing', and the amplitudes of the odd harmonics decrease as the *harmonic number m* increases.

Before we leave the subject of the mathematical aspects of the Fourier analysis of periodic functions, there is one important step to be taken. The representation of trigonometrical quantities in exponential form was discussed in Chapter 3; we will now see that Fourier's Theorem can be recast in this form with considerable advantage.

Let us go back to the theorem as originally stated in **6.2**;

$$g(t) = \sum_{n=0}^{\infty} A_n \cos(2\pi nf_0 t + \phi_n).$$
[6.2]

Since $\cos\theta = \frac{1}{2}[\exp i\theta + \exp(-i\theta)]$, we can immediately express **6.2** as

$$g(t) = \frac{1}{2} \sum_{n=0}^{\infty} A_n \exp(2\pi inf_0 t)\exp i\phi_n + \frac{1}{2} \sum_{n=0}^{\infty} A_n \exp(-2\pi inf_0 t)\exp(-i\phi_n).$$
6.9

If we change the sign of n wherever it occurs in the second summation in **6.9**, this summation takes the form

$$\frac{1}{2} \sum_{n=-\infty}^{0} A_n \exp(2\pi inf_0 t)\exp(-i\phi_{-n}).$$

We can now rewrite **6.9** as

$$g(t) = \frac{1}{2}A_0 \exp i\phi_0 + \frac{1}{2}A_0 \exp(-i\phi_0) + \sum_{n=1}^{\infty} \frac{1}{2}A_n \exp(2\pi inf_0 t)\exp i\phi_n +$$

$$+ \sum_{n=-\infty}^{-1} \frac{1}{2}A_n \exp(2\pi inf_0 t)\exp(-i\phi_{-n}),$$

where we have taken the two A_0 terms out of the summations. The next step is to redefine our notation in order to make the last equation more compact. We make three definitions for three different ranges of n, as follows. When $n = 0$, we let

$$G_0 = \frac{1}{2}A_0 \exp i\phi_0 + \frac{1}{2}A_0 \exp(-i\phi_0),$$

when $n > 0$, we let

$G_n = \frac{1}{2}A_n \exp i\phi_n$

and when $n < 0$, we let

$G_n = \frac{1}{2}A_{-n} \exp(-i\phi_{-n})$.

Using these definitions we see immediately that

$$g(t) = \sum_{n=-\infty}^{\infty} G_n \exp 2\pi i n f_0\, t. \tag{6.10}$$

Equation **6.10** is the complex form of Fourier's theorem, where the components are of negative as well as positive frequencies. The concept of negative frequencies may give some difficulty, but this is due to the way in which we are now analysing $g(t)$. Previously the frequency components were of the form $\cos 2\pi n f_0\, t$ and $\sin 2\pi n f_0\, t$ which, because n is non-negative, were always considered as of positive frequency. But each cosine (or sine) term can be regarded as having both a positive- and negative-frequency component since

$\cos 2\pi n f_0\, t = \frac{1}{2}[\exp 2\pi i n f_0\, t + \exp(-2\pi i n f_0\, t)]$

(with a similar identity for $\sin 2\pi n f_0\, t$), and now that we are *explicitly* using exponential functions we have to include components of negative frequencies.

To obtain the complex coefficients G_n we proceed much as we did previously to obtain S_n and C_n. We multiply **6.10** by

$\exp(-2\pi i m f_0\, t)\, dt$,

where m is an integer (this time positive, negative or zero), integrate over a whole period of the function $g(t)$ to obtain

$$\int_{-1/2f_0}^{+1/2f_0} g(t)\exp(-2\pi i m f_0\, t)\, dt = \int_{-1/2f_0}^{+1/2f_0} \exp(-2\pi i m f_0\, t) \sum_{n=-\infty}^{\infty} G_n \exp 2\pi i n f_0\, t\, dt. \tag{6.11}$$

(It will be noticed that the limits of integration have been changed; we are quite at liberty to do this provided we always integrate over a whole period.) A typical term on the right-hand side of **6.11** is

$$G_n \int_{-1/2f_0}^{+1/2f_0} \exp 2\pi i(n-m) f_0\, t\, dt = G_n \left[\frac{\exp 2\pi i(n-m) f_0\, t}{2\pi i(n-m) f_0} \right]_{-1/2f_0}^{+1/2f_0}$$

$$= \frac{G_n}{2\pi i(n-m) f_0} [\exp i\pi(n-m) - \exp\{-i\pi(n-m)\}]$$

$$= \frac{G_n}{\pi(n-m) f_0} \frac{\exp i\pi(n-m) - \exp\{-i\pi(n-m)\}}{2i}$$

and, since $\dfrac{\exp i\theta - \exp(-i\theta)}{2i} = \sin\theta$,

this becomes $\dfrac{G_n}{\pi(n-m)f_0}\sin\pi(n-m) = 0$ if $n - m \neq 0$.

So we see, as before, that if $n - m$ is not equal to zero, a typical term on the right-hand side of **6.11** is zero. For the case $n - m = 0$, we note that, since $\sin\theta \to \theta$ as $\theta \to 0$,

$$\frac{G_n}{\pi(n-m)f_0}\sin\pi(n-m) \to \frac{G_n}{\pi(n-m)f_0}\pi(n-m) = \frac{G_n}{f_0}.$$

Thus **6.11** becomes

$$\int_{-1/2f_0}^{+1/2f_0} g(t)\,\exp(-2\pi i m f_0 t)\,dt = \frac{G_m}{f_0},$$

so the mth coefficient is

$$G_m = f_0 \int_{-1/2f_0}^{+1/2f_0} g(t)\exp(-2\pi i m f_0 t)\,dt. \qquad\qquad \textbf{6.12}$$

Equation **6.12** enables us to obtain all the Fourier coefficients for a given $g(t)$ by just one integration instead of the previous two. The reader may find it instructive to use **6.10** and **6.12** to Fourier-analyse the 'battlement' function treated previously.

2 The physical significance of Fourier's theorem

Now that we have seen how to analyse a periodic function of time into its frequency components, we must enquire rather more deeply into the significance of the operation. Fourier theory has most of its applications to mechanical, electrical and other systems which have the properties of *linearity* and *time-invariance*. The response of the system (which may be displacement, current or some other quantity) to a stimulus (which may be a force or an e.m.f. varying with time) is governed, in general, by a differential equation connecting the response to the stimulus. If this equation is linear, the system is described as *linear* with respect to the quantities being considered; if the coefficients in the equation are constants, independent of time, the system is said to be *time-invariant*. Many systems studied in physics possess these two qualities to very good approximations. As an example, a mechanical system whose displacement can be characterized by a variable $y(t)$, impressed with a sinusoidally varying force

$F \sin(2\pi ft + \epsilon)$

might be described by the equation

$$a\,\frac{d^2y}{dt^2} + b\,\frac{dy}{dt} + cy = F\sin(2\pi ft + \epsilon),$$

where a, b and c are constants. Such a system would be linear, because of the linearity of the dependent variable y, and time-invariant because of the constancy of the coefficients a, b and c.

It can be shown that the solution to the equation (assuming that the stimulus persists for all positive and negative values of t) is of the form

$$y = A\sin(2\pi ft + \phi),$$

where A and ϕ are constants determined entirely by a, b, c, F and f. This is a most important result. It states that the response y to a force F varying sinusoidally with time *itself* varies sinusoidally with time at the same frequency. Suppose the input force were of the form

$$F_1\sin(2\pi f_1 t + \epsilon_1) + F_2\sin(2\pi f_2 t + \epsilon_2);$$

then, since the equation is linear, we can use the principle of superposition to show that y is of the form

$$y = A_1\sin(2\pi f_1 t + \phi_1) + A_2\sin(2\pi f_2 t + \phi_2)$$

and so on, for any number of frequency components in the stimulus.

Thus an input stimulus of a given frequency spectrum can only produce a response with a spectrum containing *the same frequencies*. No new frequencies can be generated. Each frequency component may be modified in both phase and amplitude, but the frequencies in the output are still those of the input. If we know the Fourier coefficients of the components in the stimulus and also know how the system modifies these, then we can determine the coefficients of the spectral components in the response, and, using equation **6.10**, synthesize the waveform of the response. So, Fourier analysis of a periodic waveform turns out to be a very significant analysis in this case, since a sinusoidal variation has an *invariance*, with respect to a linear system, which no other wave shape possesses.

There are, of course, many other ways of analysing a periodic function. For many purposes a useful way is by expressing the function $g(t)$ as a power series

$$g(t) = a_0 + a_1 t + a_2 t^2 + \dots,$$

or, in a more compact notation,

$$g(t) = \sum_{m=0}^{\infty} a_m t^m.$$

If an input stimulus were analysed in this way, the principle of superposition would still hold in that the response of the system to each individual component of the stimulus in the power series could be determined, and the effects of each term added to synthesize the final response. But the operation would be much more complex; one term in the power series, say $a_3 t^3$, would generate not only the cubic term in the response, but a whole power series, as would all the other components. On the other hand, if the original $g(t)$ had been *Fourier-analysed*, each component frequency in the stimulus would have produced that, and only that, frequency component in the response.

These processes of *frequency* analysis and synthesis are important in, for example, audio systems. When we buy our high-fidelity reproduction equipment, we demand of the manufacturer that the amplifier and loudspeaker be able to transmit the entire audio range of frequencies to our ears. Since we can hear sounds of frequencies up to 15 000 Hz, and our tapes and records contain frequencies up to that value, we require that the system does not modify the amplitude of the Fourier components in that range.

Fourier analysis is, then, a most useful concept in wave theory, and before passing on to more applications of it we must see how the theory can be generalized still further to include non-periodic signals.

6.3   The Fourier transform

Many of the uses to which waves are put are in the field of communications; for example light waves communicate information to our eyes, sound waves to our ears and radio waves allow information to be broadcast over large distances. It is immediately evident that the information being transmitted is not, in general, a periodically repeating function; this section will deal with the frequency analysis of those signals which are not of the simple periodic type so far described in this chapter.

There are many approaches to this problem; let it be said at the outset that a rigorous approach is mathematically very complex and far outside the scope of this book. Instead, we shall give an exposition which will indicate the plausibility of the theory, but which will probably not appeal to the mathematical purist.

We start with **6.10**, which is the complex form of Fourier's theorem for periodic functions,

$$g(t) = \sum_{n=-\infty}^{\infty} G_n \exp 2\pi i n f_0 t, \qquad [6.10]$$

together with the equation **6.12**, for determining the coefficients G_n of the series,

$$G_n = f_0 \int_{-1/2f_0}^{+1/2f_0} g(t) \exp(-2\pi i n f_0 t) \, dt, \qquad [6.12]$$

where n has been substituted for m. Let us first consider **6.10**. A non-periodic function can be thought of as a periodic function of infinitely long period (and therefore of infinitely small fundamental frequency f_0). As the period gets longer and longer, the component frequencies become closer and closer together on the frequency scale. For example, if the period were as long as one second, the fundamental f_0 would be 1 Hz and each component would be 1 Hz apart from its neighbours. If the period is now extended to a hundred seconds, the fundamental would be 1/100 Hz and the components would be only 1/100 Hz apart in the frequency. And so, as we let the period tend to infinity, the components become infinitely close together and in the limit merge to form a continuum. Instead of the discrete frequencies nf_0, we have a continuous variable f; likewise, the G_n in **6.10** are replaced by a quantity which describes the total amplitude within an elemental frequency band of width df. Let us call this quantity $G(f)\,df$, where $G(f)$ is the total amplitude per unit frequency range at the frequency f. The summation sign now becomes an integral and **6.10** becomes

$$g(t) = \int_{-\infty}^{\infty} G(f)\exp 2\pi ift\, df. \qquad\qquad 6.13$$

So the spectrum of a non-periodic function $g(t)$ is a *continuous* spectrum described by $G(f)$ and, if we know the spectrum, we can reconstruct the function $g(t)$ from it by the integral in **6.13**.

But suppose that we know the original function $g(t)$ and wish to find its spectrum. To do this we must turn to **6.12** for periodic functions and modify it in a way similar to that which we have employed for **6.10**. If we consider the right-hand side of **6.12** as the period of $g(t)$ tends to infinity, then nf_0 is replaced (as before) by the continuous variable f, f_0 becomes df and the limits of the integral, $+1/2f_0$ and $-1/2f_0$, tend to $+\infty$ snd $-\infty$ respectively. Since G_n on the left-hand side of **6.12** is replaced by $G(f)\,df$, this equation now becomes

$$G(f) = \int_{-\infty}^{+\infty} g(t)\exp(-2\pi ift)\, dt. \qquad\qquad 6.14$$

This is the equation we employ to find the spectrum of a non-periodic function $g(t)$.

The two equations **6.13** and **6.14** represent a very general description of Fourier's theorem for functions of time. They also illustrate the essential symmetry which underlies the theorem, in that **6.14** is identical to **6.13** except that the variables t and f have been interchanged, the two functions G and g have likewise been interchanged, and the exponent is negative in one case and positive in the other. Any function $g(t)$ (with certain reservations which need not concern us here) when integrated to give its spectrum (**6.14**), which is then integrated again (**6.13**), will yield precisely the original function $g(t)$. This shows the very important point that if the spectrum $G(f)$ of a signal $g(t)$ is known completely, then the original signal $g(t)$ can be determined uniquely; if this were not so, then the process of integrating twice as described above would not be capable of generating the original function. All the *information* in the original signal is therefore preserved in its spectrum.

The function $G(f)$ is known as the *Fourier transform* (or *Fourier integral*) of the function $g(t)$. In some literature $g(t)$ and $G(f)$ are termed *Fourier mates* or *transform pairs* of each other.

To fix our ideas, let us find the Fourier transform of a signal

$$y = y_0 \cos 2\pi f_0 t,$$

which starts at time $-T$ and stops at time $+T$, as illustrated in Figure 37.

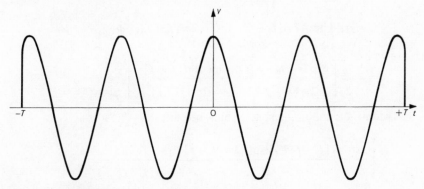

Figure 37 Cosine function extending over a finite time

One could imagine this signal as a pure sound of limited duration, such as one of the pulses which make up the Greenwich time signal. Such a signal is, of course, not periodic; it may, perhaps, be thought of as periodic between the finite time limits $-T$ and $+T$ but is certainly not so over the whole time scale. We know that if the value of T were infinity the function would extend over all time, and therefore would be truly periodic, there being only one frequency component at the frequency f_0. (Strictly speaking, of course, there would also be a component at a frequency $-f_0$, because we have chosen in our theory to include negative frequencies.) The problem now is to determine the effect on the frequency spectrum of limiting the duration of the pure tone.

To do this, we must use Fourier transforms. The function $y(t)$ that we wish to transform is characterized mathematically by the following description:

$$y(t) = \begin{cases} y_0 \cos 2\pi f_0 t & \text{for } |t| \leqslant T, \\ 0 & \text{for } |t| > T. \end{cases} \qquad \textbf{6.15}$$

The Fourier transform of $y(t)$ – let us call it $Y(f)$ – is given by **6.14**,

$$Y(f) = \int_{-\infty}^{\infty} y(t) \exp(-2\pi i f t) \, dt.$$

Since $y(t)$ is zero for t less than $-T$ and greater than $+T$, the limits of the integral now assume these time values. So

$$Y(f) = \int_{-T}^{T} y_0 \cos 2\pi f_0\, t \exp(-2\pi i f t)\, dt$$

$$= \int_{-T}^{T} y_0 \tfrac{1}{2}[\exp 2\pi i f_0\, t + \exp(-2\pi i f_0\, t)]\exp(-2\pi i f t)\, dt$$

$$= \tfrac{1}{2} y_0 \int_{-T}^{T} [\exp 2\pi i\{f_0 - f\}t + \exp(-2\pi i\{f_0 + f\}t)]\, dt$$

$$= \frac{y_0}{2} \left[\frac{\exp 2\pi i\{f_0 - f\}t}{2\pi i\{f_0 - f\}} + \frac{\exp(-2\pi i\{f_0 + f\}t)}{-2\pi i\{f_0 + f\}} \right]_{-T}^{+T},$$

which, after substitution of the limits, becomes

$$\frac{y_0}{2} \left[\frac{\exp 2\pi i\{f_0 - f\}T - \exp(-2\pi i\{f_0 - f\}T)}{2i} \frac{1}{\pi\{f_0 - f\}} - \right.$$

$$\left. \frac{\exp(-2\pi i\{f_0 + f\}T) - \exp 2\pi i\{f_0 + f\}T}{2i} \frac{1}{\pi\{f_0 + f\}} \right].$$

Since $\dfrac{\exp i\theta - \exp(-i\theta)}{2i} = \sin\theta$,

this becomes

$$Y(f) = \frac{y_0}{2} \left[\frac{\sin 2\pi(f_0 - f)T}{\pi(f_0 - f)} + \frac{\sin 2\pi(f_0 + f)T}{\pi(f_0 + f)} \right],$$

which, finally, can be put in the form

$$Y(f) = y_0 T \left[\frac{\sin 2\pi(f_0 - f)T}{2\pi(f_0 - f)T} + \frac{\sin 2\pi(f_0 + f)T}{2\pi(f_0 + f)T} \right].$$

How do we interpret this Fourier transform? First of all, we notice that each of the two terms in the brackets is of the form

$$\frac{\sin \pi x}{\pi x}$$

(sometimes called sinc x) where x in the first case is $2(f_0 - f)T$ and in the second case $2(f_0 + f)T$. The last equation can now be written in the form

$$Y(f) = y_0 T[\text{sinc}\, 2(f_0 - f)T + \text{sinc}\, 2(f_0 + f)T]. \qquad \textbf{6.16}$$

The familiar graph of sinc x against x is sketched in Figure 38.

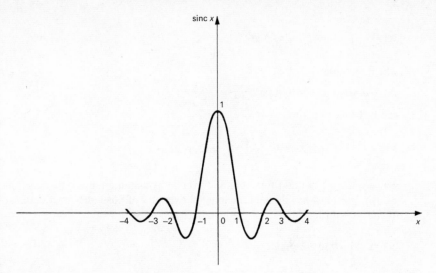

Figure 38 Graph of sinc function

A little thought will reveal that the right-hand-side of **6.16** contains two functions of this type, the first centred on the frequency f_0 and the second on $-f_0$. The transform is sketched in Figure 39.

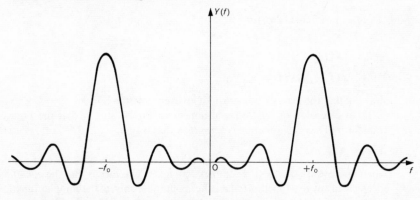

Figure 39 Fourier transform of the function shown in Figure 37

This Fourier transform, which represents the spectrum of the original pulse $y(t)$, shows a characteristic of non-periodic functions. It is a *band spectrum*; that is, unlike the spectrum in Figure 36, it exists continuously over a range of frequencies. Moreover, it is an even function. In fact, the Fourier transform of any even real function is even, as can quite easily be shown as follows. Suppose $x(t)$ is an even function of t. Then its Fourier transform, say $X(f)$, is related to $x(t)$ by

$$X(f) = \int\limits_{-\infty}^{\infty} x(t)\exp(-2\pi i f t)\, dt,$$

which, because

$$\exp(-2\pi i f t) = \cos 2\pi f t - i \sin 2\pi f t,$$

can be broken up into

$$X(f) = \int\limits_{-\infty}^{\infty} x(t)\cos 2\pi f t\, dt - i \int\limits_{-\infty}^{\infty} x(t)\sin 2\pi f t\, dt.$$

Since $\sin 2\pi f t$ is an odd function, and $x(t)$ is, by definition, even, the function $x(t)\sin 2\pi f t$ must be odd, and the integral over all t of this latter function must therefore vanish. Thus

$$X(f) = \int\limits_{-\infty}^{\infty} x(t)\cos 2\pi f t\, dt.$$

If we now substitute $-f$ for f in the integral we obtain

$$X(-f) = \int\limits_{-\infty}^{\infty} x(t)\cos(-2\pi f t)\, dt$$

$$= \int\limits_{-\infty}^{\infty} x(t)\cos(+2\pi f t)\, dt$$

$$= X(f).$$

Thus $\quad X(f) = X(-f)$,

showing that the Fourier transform of an even function is even.

By an extension of the above argument, it can be shown that the Fourier transform of *any* real function is *hermitian*, that is that

$$X(f) = X^*(-f),$$

where the asterisk denotes the complex conjugate. This means that the *amplitude spectrum* of any real function (where the magnitude, only, of the complex function is calculated) is always even. For this reason we can ignore the negative frequency range of a Fourier transform when we are interpreting it, since it provides no essentially new information.

The greatest amplitude occurs at the frequency f_0 of the pulse. However, the shortness of duration of the pulse has introduced more frequency components around the frequency f_0. In fact, examination of **6.16** shows that the shorter the total duration, $2T$, of the pulse, the broader will be the sinc function. Conversely, the longer the duration (i.e. the closer $y(t)$ is to the ideal infinitely extending cosine function) the narrower the sinc function becomes. Figure 40 illustrates

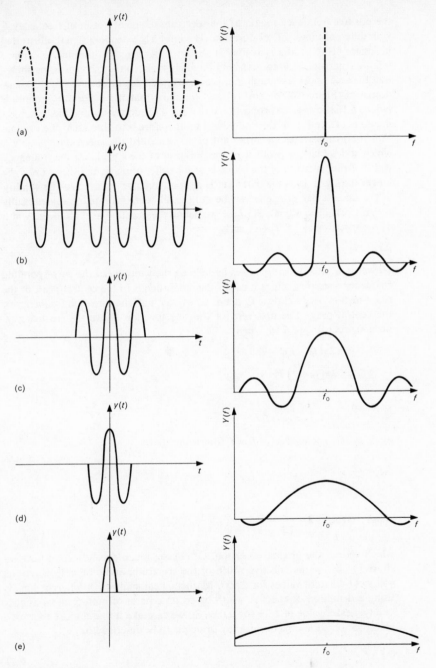

Figure 40 Effect on the Fourier transform of termination of signal

the positive frequency region of the spectrum of signals, each of frequency f_0 with different times, $2T$, of duration. The infinitely extending signal, illustrated in Figure 41(a), produces a 'line' spectrum – that is to say, the sinc function is infinitely narrow, centred on f_0 and infinitely high. (It may, however, be shown that the area under the graph in this case is finite.) As the duration of the signal decreases, Figures 40(b), (c), (d) and (e) show that the maximum amplitude (which **6.16** shows to be proportional to T) of $Y(f)$ decreases, and the broadness increases. The effect of the finite duration therefore is to 'broaden' the original 'line'. This illustrates an important principle, called the *uncertainty principle*, which states that the product of the duration of the signal and the frequency width of the spectrum of the signal is of the order of unity. In other words, the longer the signal lasts the narrower is its spectrum and vice versa. The validity of the uncertainty principle can be quite easily demonstrated mathematically for this particular signal. Suppose we define the duration as Δt and the width of the spectrum as Δf. Then clearly

$$\Delta t = 2T.$$

However, a little difficulty arises in defining the width Δf of the corresponding frequency spectrum. Since most of the amplitude is in the central peak of the sinc function, let us choose to define Δf as, say, half the spread in frequency of the central peak. The first zero of the sinc function above the frequency f_0 occurs, according to **6.16**, when

$$\sin 2\pi(f_0 - f)T = 0,$$

i.e. when $\quad 2\pi(f_0 - f)T = \pi$

or when $\qquad f_0 - f = \dfrac{1}{2T}.$

Since we have defined Δf as $f_0 - f$, this means that

$$\Delta f = \frac{1}{2T}.$$

Thus $\quad \Delta t \Delta f = 2T\,\dfrac{1}{2T} = 1,$

which verifies the original assertion. Of course, much depends upon how we choose to define the effective width of the spectrum, and different definitions will yield different values for $\Delta t \Delta f$. Mathematical analyses of different signals using a definition of effective width based on criteria of more general applicability yield a value of $1/2\pi$ for $\Delta f \Delta t$. So we can take it that a more thorough investigation shows the uncertainty principle to be described by

$$\Delta t \Delta f = \frac{1}{2\pi}.$$

6.17

However, the important point is that the number on the right-hand side of **6.17** is not zero, that there does exist, as a consequence of the nature of time and frequency, this connection between one and the other. We shall be returning to this point in Chapter 10.

The delta function

In connection with the uncertainty principle and with many other topics related to Fourier transforms, an important concept is that of the *delta function*, introduced first by P. A. M. Dirac and described in his famous book *The Principles of Quantum Mechanics* (Clarendon Press, 4th edn, 1958, pp. 58–61). The delta function may be considered as describing the spectrum of the cosine function as its duration $2T$ tends to infinity. The nearer this limit of duration is approached, the narrower the spectrum becomes (according to the uncertainty principle) until, when the cosine function is infinitely extended, the spectrum is of infinitesimal width and becomes an example of what is known as a *line spectrum*. The entity describing such a limiting situation is the delta function, which we may regard, therefore, as a limiting case of a sinc function. However, it turns out that a simpler (and equally valid) approach is to consider it as the limit of a different function which is illustrated in Figure 41. This is a function $y(x)$ which

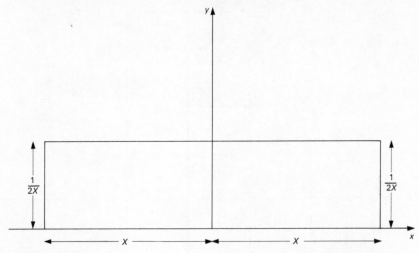

Figure 41 The function
$$y(x) = 0 \qquad |x| > X$$
$$ = \frac{1}{2x} \qquad |x| \leqslant X$$

is equal to zero for distances greater than some value X on either side of the origin of x, and to $1/2X$ for distances less than X. In other words,

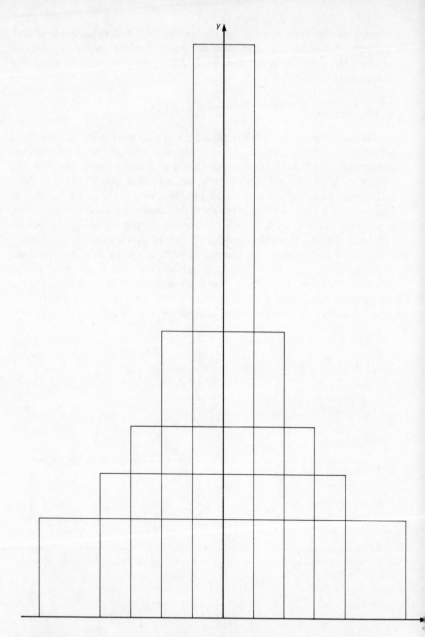

Figure 42 The function described by equations **6.18** for different values of X. Each rectangle is of unit area, but the width decreases as X decreases. In the limit of $X = 0$, the width is infinitesimal and the height infinite; the integrated area, however, is still unity

$$y(x) = \begin{cases} 0 & |x| > X, \\ \dfrac{1}{2X} & |x| \leqslant X. \end{cases} \qquad\qquad \textbf{6.18}$$

These values have been chosen so that the integrated area,

$$\int_{-\infty}^{+\infty} y(x)\, dx$$

is unity, since, clearly, this is equal to the product of the height $1/2X$ of the rectangle and its width $2X$. This integrated area is therefore independent of the value of X. Let us now investigate what happens when we let X tend to zero. The height of the function will increase, and its width will shrink until, in the limit, the width will be infinitesimal and the height infinite. The integrated area, however, will still be unity. Figure 42 shows how the limit is approached. We define the delta function to be the limiting case of $y(x)$ as X tends to zero, and we denote the function by the symbol $\delta(x)$. Thus

$$\delta(x) = \lim_{X \to 0} y(x).$$

The symbol $\delta(x)$ should not be confused with δx meaning a small finite increment of x. The brackets after the δ-symbol should eliminate this ambiguity. The symbol $\delta(x)$ is defined as describing a delta function situated at that point on the x-axis for which the quantity in brackets is equal to zero. So, for example, the symbol $\delta(x - a)$ is the mathematical description of a delta function at the point $x = a$, and, by the same reasoning, $\delta(x)$ represents a delta function at $x = 0$.

For certain applications we may wish to specify a delta function, at a particular value of x, of integrated area other than unity; all we need do in this case, of course, is to multiply the delta function by the appropriate amount. Thus, if we wish to specify a delta function of integrated area 2 and situated at $x = -3$, we write $2\delta(x + 3)$. A convenient method of representing delta functions graphically is by drawing a vertical line of height proportional to the integrated area. Some examples are given in Figure 43.

Let us now see how the delta-function concept works in a simple, but very important, case. We suspect, from our previous discussion on the uncertainty principle, that the Fourier transform of $\cos 2\pi f_0 t$ (where the function has infinite duration for positive and negative time) consists of a delta function at the value f_0 along the f-axis and another of equal magnitude at the value $-f_0$. We do not know what the magnitude is; let us therefore call it A. Now if we tackled the problem directly by applying **6.14** we would see that the Fourier transform of $\cos 2\pi f_0 t$ is

$$\int_{-\infty}^{\infty} \cos 2\pi f_0 t \exp(-2\pi i f t)\, dt,$$

1   The Delta Function

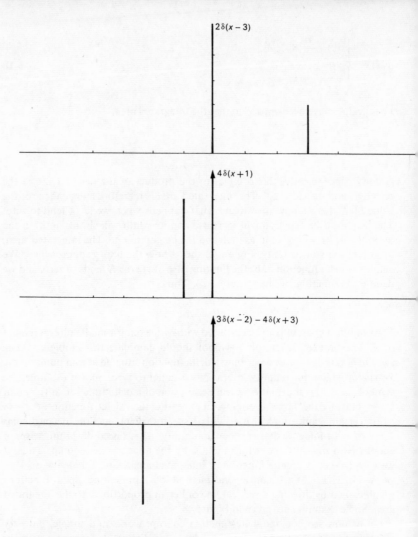

Figure 43 Some examples of delta functions and their graphical representation. The heights of the lines representing the delta functions are proportional to their integrated areas. In (c) there are two delta functions on one graph, and the one at $x = -3$ is of magnitude -4

but we cannot go further than this because the integral cannot be evaluated straightforwardly. However, assuming, as we have done, that the Fourier transform is

$$A[\delta(f - f_0) + \delta(f + f_0)], \qquad \text{6.19}$$

we can transform back into time from frequency and see if we obtain the function $\cos 2\pi f_0 t$. To do this we use **6.13**, substituting the expression **6.19** for $G(f)$. So $g(t)$ is given by

$$g(t) = \int\limits_{-\infty}^{\infty} A[\delta(f - f_0) + \delta(f + f_0)]\exp 2\pi ift \, df,$$

which can be expressed as the sum of two terms, so that

$$g(t) = A \int\limits_{-\infty}^{\infty} \delta(f - f_0)\exp 2\pi ift \, df + A \int\limits_{-\infty}^{\infty} \delta(f + f_0)\exp 2\pi ift \, df.$$

Let us consider the first integral: $\delta(f - f_0)$ is zero everywhere except at $f = f_0$, so the only contribution that $\exp 2\pi ift$ can make to the integral is for $f = f_0$. Also, since the integrated area of the delta function is unity, the integral becomes $A\exp 2\pi if_0 t$. Similarly, the second integral is $A\exp(-2\pi if_0 t)$; thus the full equation now becomes

$$g(t) = A[\exp 2\pi if_0 t + \exp(-2\pi if_0 t)].$$

Furthermore, since $\cos\theta = \frac{1}{2}[\exp i\theta + \exp(-i\theta)]$,

$$g(t) = 2A \cos 2\pi f_0 t.$$

Putting $A = \frac{1}{2}$ in expression **6.19**, we see that $g(t)$ is, indeed, $\cos 2\pi f_0 t$. Thus the Fourier transform of $\cos 2\pi f_0 t$ is

$$\tfrac{1}{2}\delta(f - f_0) + \tfrac{1}{2}\delta(f + f_0). \qquad\qquad\qquad \textbf{6.20}$$

The transform pair is illustrated in Figure 44.

An interesting fact emerges when we make f_0 zero. The function $\cos 2\pi f_0 t$ becomes unity over all time and its Fourier transform becomes

$$\tfrac{1}{2}\delta(f - 0) + \tfrac{1}{2}\delta(f + 0) = \delta(f),$$

that is, a delta function at the origin. In other words, a steady d.c. voltage has a spectrum entirely at the zero of frequency. Furthermore, by using the symmetry of t and f in the transform relationship as described in an earlier section, we see that the Fourier transform of $\delta(t)$ is unity for all frequencies. In other words, the spectrum of a sharp pulse contains equal amplitude at all frequencies.

We now see more clearly the nature of the delta function. It is not a description of anything that could exist in nature but it is a very useful idealization. No signal of the description $\cos 2\pi f_0 t$ can be produced by any apparatus, since such apparatus would need to have been made (and switched on) an infinite time ago, and moreover would have to continue to operate for an infinite time to come. Consequently, there can be no spectra consisting of delta functions. Nevertheless, in practice we can get very close to the line-spectrum situation which makes the concept important.

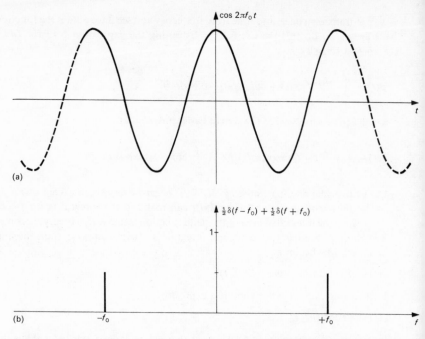

Figure 44 (a) The function $\cos 2\pi f_0 t$, and (b) its Fourier transform

The delta-function is by no means limited to discussions on Fourier transforms; it is unconsciously built in to our thinking at an early age. The particle of classical mechanics is introduced as a body having a finite mass but no size. It is the limiting case of a finite-sized body of mass m as the size tends to zero, the density meanwhile tending to infinity in such a way as to keep the total mass m a constant. In other words, the particle is none other than a three-dimensional version of a delta function of magnitude m. In the same way we can treat point electric charges, and many other physical concepts, as delta functions.

We shall now see that the spectra of periodic functions can be regarded from the point of view of Fourier transforms rather than Fourier series. The Fourier transform of a periodic function consists of a series of equally spaced delta functions f_0 apart in frequency. This can be demonstrated quite simply. Consider a function $g(t)$ (not necessarily periodic). Its Fourier transform is

$$G(f) = \int_{-\infty}^{\infty} g(t)\exp(-2\pi i f t)\, dt. \qquad \textbf{6.21}$$

The same function shifted along the time axis by a constant time τ is $g(t + \tau)$. If this has a Fourier transform $G_1(f)$ say, then

$$G_1(f) = \int\limits_{-\infty}^{\infty} g(t + \tau)\exp(-2\pi ift)\ dt.$$

Putting $t + \tau = u$, we have

$$G_1(f) = \int\limits_{-\infty}^{\infty} g(u)\exp[-2\pi if(u - \tau)]\ du.$$

Since τ is a constant, the factor $\exp 2\pi if\tau$ can be taken outside the integral which therefore becomes

$$G_1(f) = \exp 2\pi if\tau \int\limits_{-\infty}^{\infty} g(u)\exp(-2\pi ifu)\ du.$$

The integral itself is now identical to that in **6.21**, except that the variable is u and not t. This makes no difference whatsoever to the value of a definite integral; therefore, if we substitute the left-hand side of **6.21** for the integral, we obtain

$$G_1(f) = \exp 2\pi if\tau\ G(f).$$

[This is a useful general theorem in Fourier-transform theory called the *shift theorem*; if the Fourier transform of $g(t)$ is $G(f)$, then the Fourier transform of $g(t + \tau)$ is $\exp 2\pi if\tau G(f)$.] Suppose now that $g(t)$ is a periodic function with period τ. Then

$$g(t) = g(t + \tau)$$
and therefore $\quad G(f) = \exp 2\pi if\tau\ G(f).$ **6.22**

Equation **6.22** defines some of the essential properties of Fourier transforms of periodic functions. Suppose we consider those values of the frequency f for which the exponential in **6.22** is equal to unity. These values are those for which the exponent is equal to $2\pi ni$ (n is a positive, negative or zero integer), and thus are given by

$$2\pi if\tau = 2\pi ni$$
or $\quad f\tau = n,$

i.e. $f = \dfrac{n}{\tau}$

$$= \dots, -\frac{2}{\tau}, -\frac{1}{\tau}, 0, +\frac{1}{\tau}, +\frac{2}{\tau}, \dots. \qquad \textbf{6.23}$$

For these values of f, and these values only, **6.22** is a self-evident identity, since it reduces to $G(f) = G(f)$. But for *any other* values of f, **6.22** can only be true if $G(f) = 0$. Thus the Fourier transform of a periodic function is everywhere zero except at those values of frequency given by **6.23**, at which values there are delta functions. These delta functions have magnitudes equal to those given by **6.12** (although we have not shown this).

We have dealt in this chapter with the bases of Fourier analysis and synthesis. In the ensuing chapters we shall see something of the manifold applications of this elegant theory.

Chapter 7
Some Wave Phenomena

The Doppler effect

When a source of waves and an observer are moving relative to one another, the observer receives a wave of frequency different from that of the wave received when source and observer are at rest. Also, the frequency changes as the relative velocity changes. This phenomenon is known as the Doppler effect, and a common acoustical example of it is the change in the pitch of the note of the horn sounded by a passing vehicle.

We shall deduce expressions for the magnitude of this effect. Consider first a source S, initially at rest, emitting a wave of frequency f, which propagates with wavelength λ and wave velocity c, and which is received by an observer O, also initially at rest (Figure 45). We assume that the medium is at rest, and consider motion only in one dimension (i.e. along SO in Figure 45).

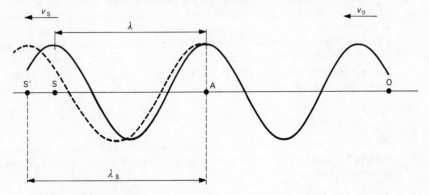

Figure 45 Doppler effect in one dimension

When both S and O are at rest, the number of wave crests received by O in unit time is equal to the frequency f of the wave. Suppose now that O moves towards S with a constant speed v_O; the number of crests received by O in unit time will be increased by the number of crests that are contained in a length equal to the distance travelled by O in unit time.

Since this distance is v_O, and the distance between adjacent crests is the wavelength λ, the number of extra crests received by O is v_O/λ. Thus if f_O is the apparent frequency received by O, we have

$$f_O = f + \frac{v_O}{\lambda}.$$

But, since $\qquad c = f\lambda,$ [3.20]

we have $\quad f_O = f + \frac{v_O f}{c}.$

Thus $\qquad f_O = f\, \frac{c + v_O}{c}.$

If O moves to the right with speed v_O, it will receive v_O/λ fewer crests in unit time, so the apparent frequency of the received wave will be

$$f_O = f\, \frac{c - v_O}{c}. \qquad\qquad 7.1$$

If we define velocity to be positive when movement is from left to right, and negative when movement is from right to left then 7.1 covers both situations, provided the numerical value of v_O is inserted with the correct sign.

Next we examine the effect of the motion of the source. When the source is at rest, successive wave crests emitted by it are one wavelength λ apart, but when the source is moving away from the observer, the distance between adjacent crests is increased by the distance the source travels in one cycle. The situation is shown in Figure 45, in which S is moving to the left with constant speed v_S; the distance travelled by S in one cycle is SS' and the wavelength is increased from SA $(=\lambda)$ for stationary S to S'A $(=\lambda_S)$. The time taken for one cycle is $1/f$ and the velocity of S is v_S; the distance SS' is thus v_S/f. Therefore

$$\lambda_S = \lambda + \frac{v_S}{f}. \qquad\qquad 7.2$$

But since the medium in which the wave is being propagated is at rest, the wave velocity is unchanged, so that the frequency of the signal received by the stationary observer is

$$f_S = \frac{c}{\lambda_S}.$$

Replacing λ_S and λ in 7.2 by c/f_S and c/f respectively, we have

$$\frac{c}{f_S} = \frac{c}{f} + \frac{v_S}{f};$$

thus $\quad f_S = \frac{cf}{c + v_S}.$

Similarly, for S moving from left to right, the wavelength is shortened by the distance travelled by S during one cycle, and the observed frequency is given by

$$f_s = \frac{cf}{c - v_s} \, . \qquad\qquad 7.3$$

We shall adopt the same sign convention as for v_o (positive when moving toward the right) so **7.3** covers both cases when v_s is given the appropriate sign.

These results can be combined as follows to give the frequency f_{o+s} received by the observer when both source and observer are in motion. The moving source gives rise to a wave whose apparent frequency is given by **7.3**. If we take f_s to be the frequency of the wave itself, we need not concern ourselves further with the source. The moving observer will receive a wave whose apparent frequency, f_{o+s}, is obtained by substituting f_s for f in the right-hand side of **7.1**, giving

$$f_{o+s} = f \, \frac{c - v_o}{c - v_s} \, .$$

Perhaps the most interesting example of the Doppler effect is in astronomy. When the light from a star is examined spectroscopically, it is found to contain the spectra of common terrestrial elements, but the spectral lines are shifted towards the red end of the spectrum (i.e. the values of λ are all greater than those found in the laboratory). This 'red shift' can be explained by **7.2**, for if the star is travelling away from the earth, it is evident that $\lambda_s > \lambda$. However, the truth is rather more complex than this since, firstly, **7.2** is only approximately true for light waves and, secondly, there are other agencies which cause a red shift.

.2 Dispersion and group velocity

Each physical system treated in Chapter 4 gave a unique wave speed determined solely by the physical constants of the medium concerned. We found that

$$c = \sqrt{\frac{T}{\mu}}$$

for a string, and

$$c = \sqrt{\frac{K}{\rho_0}}$$

for a fluid, so that waves can be propagated with these speeds and with no others.

There are, however, examples in physics in which the wave velocity turns out to be dependent upon the wavelength, but these are considerably more difficult to treat than those of Chapter 4. One example is that of surface waves on a liquid of depth h, density ρ and surface tension γ for which

$$c^2 = \left[\frac{g}{2\pi k} + \frac{2\pi\gamma k}{\rho} \right] \tanh(2\pi kh),$$

where g is the acceleration due to gravity and k is the wave number. Another example is that of light waves in a transparent medium, where the relationship between c and λ is rather complicated, but can be expressed approximately by

$$\frac{1}{c} = A + \frac{B}{\lambda^2},$$

where A and B are constants for the medium concerned. This property of velocity dependence upon wavelength is called *dispersion*; a medium possessing this property is called a *dispersive medium*.

We now proceed to examine the collective behaviour of a number of waves of different wavelength propagated simultaneously through a medium. We saw in Chapter 5 how two or more waves may be superposed according to the principle of superposition. There we superposed two waves of the same frequency and wave number; let us now see what happens when we superpose two waves of slightly different frequency and wave number, but of the same amplitude.

Let the two waves be

$$y_1 = a \sin 2\pi(f_1 t - k_1 x)$$
$$\text{and} \quad y_2 = a \sin 2\pi(f_2 t - k_2 x).$$

Then, according to the principle of superposition, the combined effect of these two waves is given by

$$y = y_1 + y_2$$
$$= 2a \sin 2\pi[\tfrac{1}{2}(f_1 + f_2)t - \tfrac{1}{2}(k_1 + k_2)x] \cos 2\pi[\tfrac{1}{2}(f_1 - f_2)t - \tfrac{1}{2}(k_1 - k_2)x]. \qquad \textbf{7.4}$$

The sine term represents a wave whose frequency and wave number are the averages of those of the original wave, and whose wave velocity is

$$\frac{f_1 + f_2}{k_1 + k_2}.$$

Since we have assumed that f_1 differs only slightly from f_2, and k_1 only slightly from k_2, $\tfrac{1}{2}(f_1 + f_2)$ will differ only slightly from f_1 or f_2, and $\tfrac{1}{2}(k_1 + k_2)$ only slightly from k_1 or k_2. Thus the sine term represents a wave whose phase is very similar to those of both the original waves.

The cosine term represents a wave whose frequency and wave number are, respectively, $\tfrac{1}{2}(f_1 - f_2)$ and $\tfrac{1}{2}(k_1 - k_2)$, and whose wave velocity is therefore

$$\frac{f_1 - f_2}{k_1 - k_2};$$

this term varies more slowly with both time and distance than does the sine term. Figure 46 shows how a sketch of the function **7.4** is obtained for fixed t;

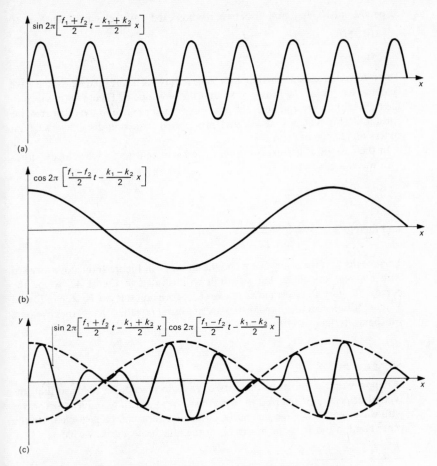

Figure 46 Superposition at constant t of two waves of slightly different f and k: (a) shows the sine term of **7.4**, (b) the cosine term, and (c) the product of the two terms (heavy line)

the ordinates of the sine term (a) and the cosine term (b) are multiplied together, point by point, to produce the heavy curve in (c) which is seen to be contained within an envelope defined by the cosine curve of (b) and its image in the x-axis. It may be seen from the symmetry between the x- and t-terms in **7.4** that a plot of y against t for constant x would give a curve of the same form as that in Figure 46(c). The successive building up and dying away of amplitude with time is the phenomenon of beats which has already been referred to at the end of Chapter 2.

A combination of two or more waves in this manner is known as a *wave group*. We will examine now how wave groups behave in non-dispersive and dispersive media. In a non-dispersive medium, the wave velocity is constant, so

$$c = \frac{f_1}{k_1} = \frac{f_2}{k_2} = \frac{f_1 + f_2}{k_1 + k_2} = \frac{f_1 - f_2}{k_1 - k_2} \, .$$

This means that the sine part and the cosine part of **7.4** have exactly the same wave velocity, so that as the heavy curve and the envelope of Figure 46(c) move to the right with increasing time, the position of each relative to the other remains constant. This means that a signal propagated in a non-dispersive medium suffers no change of form.

In the case of a dispersive medium, we have seen that wave velocity varies with wavelength so that

$$\frac{f_1}{k_1} \neq \frac{f_2}{k_2}$$

and therefore $\quad \dfrac{f_1 + f_2}{k_1 + k_2} \neq \dfrac{f_1 - f_2}{k_1 - k_2} \, .$

This means that the heavy curve and the envelope in Figure 46(c) move forward with *different* velocities. The situation is illustrated in Figure 47, where the curves of Figure 46(c) are shown at two successive times. It can be seen in Figure 47 that the inner curve is moving forward at a faster rate than that of the envelope, which means that in this example

$$\frac{f_1 - f_2}{k_1 - k_2} < \frac{f_1 + f_2}{k_1 + k_2} \, . \qquad\qquad\qquad \textbf{7.5}$$

It happens that in the great majority of cases in physics **7.5** holds so that this type of dispersion is referred to as *normal dispersion*; an example is sea waves with wavelengths so large that surface-tension effects can be neglected. On the other hand, if the envelope moves faster than the heavy curve, we have

$$\frac{f_1 - f_2}{k_1 - k_2} > \frac{f_1 + f_2}{k_1 + k_2} \, .$$

This happens less frequently in physics and is referred to as *anomalous dispersion*; examples of it are transverse waves in a solid rod and electromagnetic waves near what is known as an 'absorption edge'.

An extremely important quantity, which we must now examine, is the velocity with which energy is carried forward when two waves are superposed to form a group. When we have a single wave, the energy is carried forward with the velocity at which an amplitude maximum moves forward, which, of course, is the wave velocity. In the case of a wave group, however, we can see from a study of Figure 47 that the velocity with which an amplitude maximum moves forward is that of the *envelope*. It follows that the energy is borne forward with the

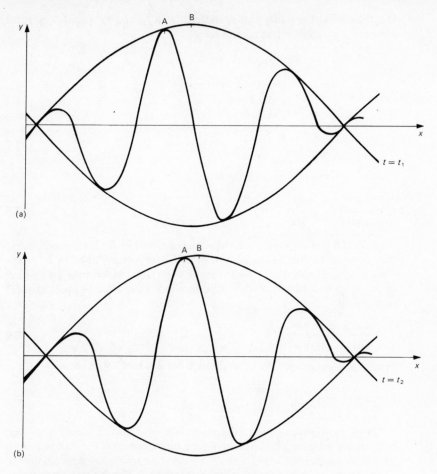

Figure 47 Wave group in a dispersive medium. The sketches (a) and (b) show the curves of Figure 46(c) at two successive instants of time. It can be seen that the crest A of the inner curve has advanced a greater distance along the x-axis than has the maximum B of the envelope

velocity of the envelope. This velocity is known as the *group velocity* c_g. We saw earlier that the envelope moves with velocity

$$\frac{f_1 - f_2}{k_1 - k_2},$$

so $c_g = \dfrac{f_1 - f_2}{k_1 - k_2}.$ **7.6**

We assumed at the outset that f_1 differed from f_2, and k_1 from k_2, by small amounts; we may therefore rewrite **7.6** as

$$c_g = \frac{\Delta f}{\Delta k}$$

where $\Delta f = f_1 - f_2$ and $\Delta k = k_1 - k_2$.
In the limit, as $\Delta k \to 0$ we have

$$c_g = \frac{df}{dk} ; \qquad\qquad\qquad 7.7$$

since $k = 1/\lambda$, this may be rewritten as

$$c_g = \frac{df}{d(1/\lambda)} = -\lambda^2 \frac{df}{d\lambda} . \qquad\qquad 7.8$$

Equation **7.8** is one of three useful equivalent expressions for the group velocity; the others can be obtained as follows. Firstly, if we replace f in **7.7** by kc, where c is the *wave* velocity (the waves which are superposed to form the group have velocities so near to one another than the single value c can be used), then **7.7** becomes

$$c_g = \frac{d(kc)}{dk} = c + k\frac{dc}{dk} . \qquad\qquad 7.9$$

Secondly, if we replace k by $1/\lambda$ in the right-hand side of **7.9** we obtain

$$c_g = c + \frac{1}{\lambda}\frac{dc}{d(1/\lambda)} = c - \lambda\frac{dc}{d\lambda} .$$

The above results have been deduced from the superposition of only two waves, but they are valid for a group comprising a superposition of any number – even an infinite number – of waves. To treat a group comprising an infinite number of waves satisfactorily requires the use of theorems in Fourier transform theory which are beyond the scope of this book.

7.3   **Modulation**

In the transmission of information by radio waves the original signal is not sent out directly, but is first modified by a process called *modulation*. At the receiving end the incoming wave is *demodulated*, producing a replica of the original signal. There are various types of modulation, the three most common of which, namely *amplitude modulation*, *phase modulation* and *frequency modulation*, will be described briefly in this section.

Amplitude modulation

This is a common technique used in radio communication; although once universal, it is now becoming displaced by frequency modulation. It is, however, very important in the history of radio. When no information is being transmitted, the transmitter gives out a pure sinusoidal wave known as the *carrier*. Different broadcasting stations operate at different *carrier frequencies*, each of which is characteristic of a particular station. When the input stage of the receiving set is adjusted to be at resonance with the carrier frequency, the set is said to be 'tuned' to that station. The carrier frequencies are (by audio standards) extremely high, typically in the range 0·1 MHz–100 MHz. Now suppose it is desired to send an audio signal $y(t)$ by radio. It is first necessary that the magnitude of the signal $|y(t)|$ never exceed a certain value. Let us suppose, for simplicity, that this value is unity. So $|y(t)| \leqslant 1$. The initial part of the process of amplitude modulation is to add a d.c. component to the signal, so that it is always positive. This can, of course, be achieved by adding such a component of unit amplitude. The signal has therefore now become $1 + y(t)$. The next part of the process is to feed this latter signal into a circuit which gives, as output, the product of the signal with the function describing the carrier wave, namely

$$[1 + y(t)]\cos 2\pi f_c t, \qquad\qquad\qquad 7.10$$

where f_c is the frequency of the carrier. Expression **7.10** is the form of the transmitted wave.

To understand why this should be a desirable modification of the original signal $y(t)$ before transmitting it, it is necessary to know the spectrum of expression **7.10**. Before we find this, let us take a simple example. Suppose we wish to transmit a pure tone of frequency f_p; that is, suppose

$$y(t) = \cos 2\pi f_p t.$$

Then **7.10** becomes

$$[1 + \cos 2\pi f_p t]\cos 2\pi f_c t, \qquad\qquad\qquad 7.11$$

which, by a little rearrangement involving familiar trigonometric identities, further becomes

$$\tfrac{1}{2}\cos 2\pi(f_c - f_p)t + \cos 2\pi f_c t + \tfrac{1}{2}\cos 2\pi(f_c + f_p)t.$$

The spectrum of this, obtained by Fourier transformation, is

$$\tfrac{1}{4}\delta(f - f_c + f_p) + \tfrac{1}{4}\delta(f + f_c - f_p) + \tfrac{1}{2}\delta(f - f_c) + \tfrac{1}{2}\delta(f + f_c) + \\ + \tfrac{1}{4}\delta(f - f_c - f_p) + \tfrac{1}{4}\delta(f + f_c + f_p),$$

by equation **6.20**, and is illustrated in Figure 48 together with the spectra of $\cos 2\pi f_p t$, $1 + \cos 2\pi f_p t$ and $\cos 2\pi f_c t$.

The above analysis, together with Figure 48, illustrates many of the essential properties of the amplitude-modulated carrier. We see immediately from the spectrum (h) of the transmitted signal (d) (expression **7.11**) that there is no amplitude at audio frequencies, although the original signal modulating the wave

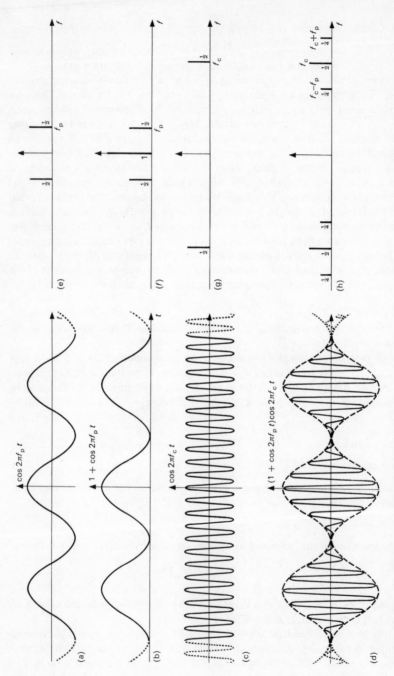

Figure 48 The functions on the left-hand side are those used in the explanation in the text of amplitude modulation; their Fourier transforms are shown on the right-hand side

is of audio frequency. This reveals the importance of modulation techniques; frequencies are *changed* from their original values to any value we care to specify, the new frequencies being determined by that of the carrier. It would in principle be possible to transmit an audio signal direct, but since we require an aerial of length of the order of λ to deliver a significant amount of power in doing so, an impractically long aerial would be needed at these frequencies. For example, to radiate efficiently a signal of 100 Hz as a radio signal we would need an aerial of length of the order of

$$\frac{\text{Velocity of light}}{\text{Frequency}} \simeq \frac{3 \times 10^8}{1000} \simeq 3 \times 10^5 \, \text{m}$$

– about two hundred miles! However, the fact that all the amplitude is concentrated at high frequencies in an amplitude-modulated signal means that an excessively long aerial is not needed for transmission. (For example at 30 MHz, λ is of the order of ten metres.)

As to the detailed structure of the spectrum in Figure 48(h), the amplitude appears to be concentrated symmetrically about the carrier frequency. This in fact is generally true, as we shall shortly show. The components represented by the delta functions at frequencies $f_c - f_p$ and $f_c + f_p$ are known as *sidebands*. The process of demodulating at the receiving end is essentially one of recovering the original spectrum from the information contained around the region of the carrier frequency. We will, however, not go into details here.

Let us now consider the Fourier transform of the function

$$[1 + y(t)]\cos 2\pi f_c \, t, \tag{7.10}$$

where $y(t)$ is a general function of time. To find this Fourier transform directly, using the techniques developed in this book, is not at all easy, but we shall adopt the same method as we did in Chapter 6 for $\cos 2\pi f_0 \, t$, namely that of anticipating what the transform might be, and working backwards. From what has already been said, the scheme sketched in Figure 49 seems a likely starting point. In (a), an arbitrary waveform designated by $y(t)$ is shown, and in (e) its Fourier transform $Y(f)$. This latter function will, in general, be complex, but the imaginary components have not been shown. Figure 49(b) shows the function $1 + y(t)$ whose transform, illustrated in (f), is the same as that of $y(t)$ except that a delta function of unit magnitude at the origin has been added. Figure 49(c) represents the carrier wave, and (g) its Fourier transform. The modulated carrier is shown in (d) and our surmise as to its Fourier transform in (h). The two delta functions in Figure 49(h) [as in Figure 48(h)] are now of magnitude $\frac{1}{2}$ and the original $Y(f)$ is scaled down in size by a factor of two, as the sidebands were in the previous example. A little thought will reveal that the function in Figure 49(h) is expressed mathematically as

$$\tfrac{1}{2}Y(f+f_c) + \tfrac{1}{2}\delta(f+f_c) + \tfrac{1}{2}Y(f-f_c) + \tfrac{1}{2}\delta(f-f_c). \tag{7.12}$$

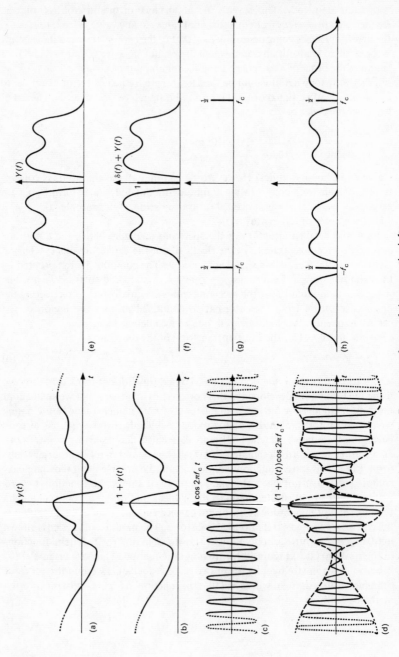

Figure 49 The functions on the right are the Fourier transforms of those on the left

Our task now is to find the inverse Fourier transform of expression **7.12**, and is basically that of answering the question of whether we can find the inverse transform of $Y(f + f_c)$ knowing that that of $Y(f)$ is $y(t)$. We can do this using the shift theorem. If we designate the inverse Fourier transform of $Y(f + f_c)$ as $y_1(t)$, then, from the shift theorem, we have

$$y_1(t) = \exp(-2\pi i f_c t) y(t)$$

(where it will be noticed that the sign of the exponent is opposite to that given in section 6.4 in the discussion on the shift theorem; this is due to the fact that we are dealing here with an *inverse* Fourier transform, that is, transforming from frequency to time). So the inverse Fourier transform of the first term in **7.12** is

$\frac{1}{2}\exp(-2\pi i f_c t) y(t)$.

Similarly, we can easily show that the inverse Fourier transform of the third term [namely $\frac{1}{2}Y(f - f_c)$] in **7.12** is $\frac{1}{2}\exp 2\pi i f_c t$. The second and fourth terms in **7.12** present no difficulty; the inverse Fourier transform of the sum of these two has already been found (**6.20**) and is $\cos 2\pi f_c t$. The inverse Fourier transform of **7.12** is thus

$$\cos 2\pi f_c t + \frac{1}{2}[\exp 2\pi i f_c t + \exp(-2\pi i f_c t)] y(t),$$

which simplifies to

$$\cos 2\pi f_c t + \cos(2\pi f_c t) y(t)$$

or $\quad [1 + y(t)]\cos 2\pi f_c t,$

which is identical to expression **7.10**. We therefore conclude that our surmise as to the Fourier transform (illustrated in Figure 49h) of expression **7.10** is correct.

From the nature of this Fourier transform we see that the bandwidth required to accommodate all the information in the original $y(t)$, when that signal is propagated as an amplitude-modulated wave, is twice the extent of the original spectrum. One of the advantages of the technique is that, by choosing appropriate carrier frequencies, the information can be propagated in whatever frequency range we choose. No interference with other information being transmitted on the same, or a neighbouring, transmitter can occur if the carrier frequencies for the two signals are sufficiently far apart in frequency.

Furthermore, it is possible to accommodate twice as many signals in a given frequency range than the above discussion would indicate by suppressing the sidebands of frequencies lower than (or higher than) that of the carrier, the information from the remaining sidebands still being extractable. This is because the amplitude spectrum is symmetrical about the carrier frequency; there is therefore no essential information about the signal in the lower sidebands that is not already contained in the upper sidebands. This *single-sideband* transmission occupies only half the bandwidth taken by the double-sideband modulation, and therefore we can put other information in the suppressed sideband region providing, of course, that the receiving set is constructed accordingly.

7.3.2   *Phase modulation and frequency modulation*

These are both examples of what is known as *angle modulation*. The signal $y(t)$, instead of modifying the amplitude of the carrier wave, as in the previous case, modifies the angle which is the argument of the cosine function representing the carrier. Without any signal, the carrier can be represented as $\cos 2\pi f_c t$; this is modified, when a signal $y(t)$ phase modulates the carrier, to $\cos[2\pi f_c t + y(t)]$. So we see that the amplitude of the carrier remains constant regardless of the presence or absence of a signal, and the information in the signal is contained in the deviation of the argument of the cosine from what it would be if $y(t)$ were zero. In a very similar way the representation of a carrier wave *frequency modulated* by a signal $y(t)$ is

$$\cos \left[2\pi f_c t + \int\limits_{-\infty}^{t} y(u)\, du \right], \hspace{2cm} \textbf{7.13}$$

where u is a dummy variable in units of time. The reason for calling **7.13** a frequency-modulated wave is as follows. We can define the *instantaneous frequency* f_i as

$$\frac{1}{2\pi} \frac{d}{dt} \quad \text{(argument of the cosine).}$$

This yields a constant value f_c for an unmodulated cosine wave $\cos 2\pi f_c t$, since the argument of the cosine here is $2\pi f_c t$, giving f_i as

$$f_i = \frac{1}{2\pi} \frac{d}{dt} (2\pi f_c t) = f_c.$$

In a similar way, we find the instantaneous frequency for the expression **7.13** is

$$f_i = \frac{1}{2\pi} \frac{d}{dt} \left[2\pi f_c t + \int\limits_{-\infty}^{t} y(u)\, du \right]$$

$$= f_c + \frac{1}{2\pi} y(t).$$

Thus $\quad f_i - f_c = \dfrac{1}{2\pi} y(t),$

and we see that the instantaneous deviation in frequency from that of the carrier is directly proportional to the magnitude of the signal at that time. Hence the wave **7.13** is described as a frequency-modulated wave.

We do not propose to go into the question of the spectra of these waves; these are much more complicated than for amplitude-modulated waves and we refer the reader who may be interested in the matter to the further reading list (for example Javid and Brenner, 1963).

Chapter 8
Sound

Introduction

This chapter is concerned with some features of sound waves. The word 'sound' has two distinct meanings. The first meaning is 'longitudinal waves in matter' – that is, the actual disturbance and its propagation in the medium; the second meaning is 'those longitudinal waves in a fluid which evoke a percept in the auditory system'. Now, as we shall discuss later in this chapter, the auditory system (i.e. the combination of ears and brain) can perceive only a limited range of frequencies. The range varies from person to person and is also dependent upon the age of a person, but is usually from about 16 Hz–16000 Hz. It is therefore evident that there can exist 'sound' in the sense of the first meaning which is certainly not sound according to the second. For this reason, physicists and others have, in recent years, referred to sounds of very low, inaudible frequencies as *infrasonic* and sounds of very high, inaudible frequencies as *ultrasonic*. But audibility is not determined solely by frequency, because, even though a sound has a spectrum within the audible frequency range, it does not necessarily mean that it can be heard. In fact for amplitudes below a certain 'threshold' the sound is too faint to be heard – i.e. the wave is not sufficiently energetic to evoke a percept.

The first observation to be made about sound in air (in its first meaning) is that it is a longitudinal wave motion that must be described by a solution of the three-dimensional equivalent of the one-dimensional wave equation

$$\frac{\partial^2 z}{\partial t^2} = c^2 \frac{\partial^2 z}{\partial x^2}$$

8.1

discussed in section 4.3.

In this equation, z is the displacement at a position x and at a time t, and c, the velocity of the sound waves, is $\sqrt{(\gamma P/\rho)}$, where γ is the ratio of principal specific heats for air, P is the ambient pressure and ρ is the density. The velocity of sound is about 330 m s^{-1} (737 m.p.h.); that is, a sound wave travels roughly one third of a kilometre in one second. Since this velocity is so much less than that of light, distant events producing simultaneous optical and acoustical disturbances (such as in an electrical storm) do not evoke simultaneous visual and aural percepts.

How does the velocity of sound vary with variations in the ambient temperature and pressure? To investigate this, we consider a fixed mass m of air, and assume it to have the properties of an ideal gas. For such a gas the ideal gas law,

$$PV = \frac{m}{M} RT,$$ 8.2

is valid. Here, V is the volume occupied at pressure P and temperature T by the mass m of the gas of molecular weight M, and R is the gas constant. The density ρ of the gas is given by the equation

$$\rho = \frac{m}{V}.$$

Substituting this into equation 8.2 we have

$$\frac{P}{\rho} = \frac{RT}{M}.$$

So the velocity c, which is equal to $\sqrt{(\gamma P/\rho)}$, becomes

$$c = \sqrt{\frac{\gamma RT}{M}}.$$ 8.3

Equation 8.3 shows that the velocity is independent of pressure and that it is proportional to the square root of the absolute temperature. These two conclusions are quite accurately true for air at ordinary temperatures and pressures, but the approximation to an ideal gas, and hence the conclusions which depend upon such an approximation, breaks down at low temperatures or high pressures.

8.2   **Sound waves in a pipe**

Sound waves within a pipe of fixed length must, of course, be described by solutions of 8.1; however, the presence of the pipe imposes boundary conditions on the problem which restrict the possible solutions, as was described in Chapter 5. Before embarking on an analysis of sound waves in pipes we make two assumptions, of which the first is that the length L of the pipe is much larger than its radius. This assumption enables us to consider the pipe as essentially a one-dimensional entity, in which the air can vibrate only along its length. We therefore r .e able to use the one-dimensional wave equation 8.1. We also assume that the pipe is of uniform cross-section.

We shall consider in detail the pipe closed at one end and open at the other. The x-axis is taken along the pipe. There are two boundary conditions that must be applied. The first is very simple; at no time can there be any displacement at the closed end of the pipe, at $x = 0$, because this is considered to be rigidly fixed. Our first boundary condition therefore is

$$[z]_{x=0} = 0 \qquad \text{for all values of } t.$$ 8.4

The second boundary condition is concerned with the magnitude of vibrations at the open end of the pipe, and is by no means as simple as the first. It will be recalled from Chapter 4 that the displacement variations in a sound wave are accompanied by pressure variations. Indeed the sound wave can be specified either by the pressure or the displacement variations, as desired. As was shown in section 4.3, the acoustic pressure p and the displacement z are related by

$$p = -K \frac{\partial z}{\partial x}. \qquad [4.5]$$

Now, because of the presence of the rigid wall of the pipe, there is no opportunity for any excess pressure caused by the displacement to dissipate in a direction perpendicular to the length of the pipe. However, beyond the open end of the pipe there is such an opportunity and, consequently, the acoustic pressure falls away very quickly. So to a first approximation we can say that there is no acoustic pressure outside the pipe. This, as we shall discuss later on, is an assumption we can make only with reservations, but it is not unreasonable. So our second boundary condition is that

$$[p]_{x=L} = 0$$

for all values of t, which, because of the equation 4.5 can be re-expressed as

$$\left[\frac{\partial z}{\partial x} \right]_{x=L} = 0 \qquad \text{for all values of } t. \qquad \textbf{8.5}$$

The wave equation **8.1**, together with the boundary conditions **8.4** and **8.5**, enable us to deduce a complete description of the wave motion within the pipe. Whatever the most general motion is, we can say from our experience in Chapter 2 that it must be some linear combination of the normal modes. Since the air in the pipe can be regarded as a continuous medium, there must be an infinite number of normal modes of vibration. Let us therefore find a typical normal-mode solution. It will be recalled that a normal-mode solution is one for which the air vibration throughout the whole pipe takes place at a single frequency, say f_n (the suffix n indicates the nth normal mode). The amplitude of vibration will vary along the length of the pipe but will, of course, be constant with time; we will describe its variation by the function $\phi_n(x)$. So a typical normal-mode solution is

$$z_n(x,t) = \phi_n(x) \cos(2\pi f_n t + \alpha_n), \qquad \textbf{8.6}$$

where α_n is a constant phase angle which belongs to the nth normal mode. Differentiating partially the equation **8.6** we obtain

$$\frac{\partial z_n}{\partial t} = -2\pi f_n \phi_n(x) \sin(2\pi f_n t + \alpha_n),$$

$$\frac{\partial^2 z_n}{\partial t^2} = -4\pi^2 f_n^2 \phi_n(x) \cos(2\pi f_n t + \alpha_n),$$

$$\frac{\partial z_n}{\partial x} = \cos(2\pi f_n t + \alpha_n)\frac{d\phi_n(x)}{dx},$$

$$\frac{\partial^2 z_n}{\partial x^2} = \cos(2\pi f_n t + \alpha_n)\frac{d^2\phi_n(x)}{dx^2}.$$

Substituting the two second derivatives into the original wave equation **8.1** we obtain

$$-4\pi^2 f_n^2 \phi_n(x)\cos(2\pi f_n t + \alpha_n) = c^2\cos(2\pi f_n t + \alpha_n)\frac{d^2\phi_n(x)}{dx^2},$$

which, after some cancellation and rearrangement, becomes

$$\frac{d^2\phi_n(x)}{dx^2} = -\frac{4\pi^2 f_n^2}{c^2}\phi_n(x). \qquad\qquad 8.7$$

Equation **8.7** is an ordinary differential equation in the one independent variable x, and we see immediately that it is identical in form to the simple-harmonic motion equation, except that the latter has t as its independent variable. The general solution of this has the form given by equation **2.3**, namely

$$\phi_n(x) = a_n \sin\left[\left(\frac{4\pi^2 f_n^2}{c^2}\right)^{1/2} x + \epsilon_n\right]$$

$$= a_n \sin\left[\frac{2\pi f_n}{c} x + \epsilon_n\right],$$

where a_n and ϵ_n are arbitrary constants which are, in general, different for different values of n. Thus the amplitude variation $\phi_n(x)$ repeats periodically at intervals of

$$\lambda_n = \pm\frac{2\pi}{2\pi f_n/c} = \pm\frac{c}{f_n}.$$

So $\quad c = \pm f_n \lambda_n.$ \qquad\qquad **8.8**

The normal-mode solution is, therefore, one of sinusoidal form (although we have not yet determined its phase) and we have shown that the wavelength λ_n is related to the frequency f_n by the simple, familiar relationship **8.8**. Since the amplitude a_n is completely arbitrary, any amplitude of vibration is possible. In other words the wave equation determines only the *form* of the wave, not its *scale*.

The typical normal-mode solution **8.6** can now be written as

$$z_n(x, t) = a_n \sin\left(\frac{2\pi f_n}{c} x + \epsilon_n\right)\cos(2\pi f_n t + \alpha_n). \qquad 8.9$$

Let us now apply the boundary condition **8.4**, namely

$$[z_n]_{x=0} = 0 \quad \text{for all } t;$$
$$z_n(0, t) = a_n \sin \epsilon_n \cos(2\pi f_n t + \alpha_n).$$

For this to be zero for all values of t, $a_n \sin \epsilon_n$ must be zero. Since $a_n = 0$ represents the trivial case of no vibration at all, we are forced to conclude that $\sin \epsilon_n$ is zero. This implies that

$$\epsilon_n = m\pi,$$

where m is an integer. The only physically distinct values of m are 0 and 1, since the angles 2π, 4π, ... are identical to 0, and 3π, 5π, ... to π. The case $\epsilon_n = \pi$ merely changes the sign of the amplitude a_n, so, without any loss of generality, we may take ϵ_n as zero. Thus, **8.9** may be rewritten as

$$z_n(x, t) = a_n \sin\left(\frac{2\pi f_n}{c} x\right) \cos(2\pi f_n t + \alpha_n). \tag{8.10}$$

To apply the second boundary condition **8.5**,

$$\left[\frac{\partial z_n}{\partial x}\right]_{x=L} = 0 \tag{8.5}$$

we must differentiate **8.10** partially with respect to x. This gives us

$$\frac{\partial z_n(x, t)}{\partial x} = a_n 2\pi \frac{f_n}{c} \cos\left(2\pi \frac{f_n}{c} x\right) \cos(2\pi f_n t + \alpha_n),$$

which, for $x = L$, becomes

$$\left[\frac{\partial z_n(x, t)}{\partial x}\right]_{x=L} = a_n 2\pi \frac{f_n}{c} \cos\left(2\pi \frac{f_n}{c} L\right) \cos(2\pi f_n t + \alpha_n).$$

But this must be zero for all values of t, by equation **8.5**, and so

$$\cos 2\pi \frac{f_n}{c} L = 0.$$

This implies that

$$2\pi \frac{f_n}{c} L = (n + \tfrac{1}{2})\pi,$$

where n is an integer, i.e.

$$\frac{f_n}{c} = \frac{(n + \tfrac{1}{2})}{2L}$$

$$= \frac{(2n + 1)}{4L}. \tag{8.11}$$

Thus the functions $\phi_n(x)$ are

$$\phi_n(x) = a_n \sin \frac{2\pi(2n + 1)x}{4L},$$

which are sine functions of wavelengths

$\lambda_0 = 4L$, $\lambda_1 = \frac{4}{3}L$, $\lambda_2 = \frac{4}{5}L$, $\lambda_3 = \frac{4}{7}L$, etc.

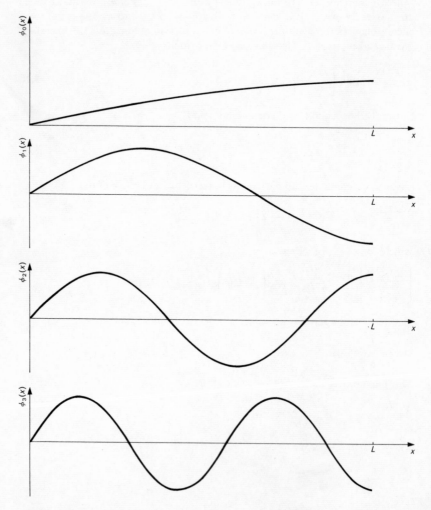

Figure 50 The first four normal modes for an open/closed pipe

The first four of these functions are sketched in Figure 50, from which it will be seen that an antinode of displacement exists at $x = L$ for all the functions ϕ_n. This is a direct consequence of the pressure node at the open end of the pipe which was the second of our boundary conditions. The displacement nodes at $x = 0$ for all the ϕ_n are, of course, a result of the boundary condition of no displacement at the closed end. The values of the different f_n are seen from **8.11** to be

$$f_n = \frac{(2n + 1)}{4L} c;$$

substituting $n = 0$ in this equation we obtain

$$f_0 = \frac{c}{4L}.$$

Similarly $\quad f_1 = 3\,\dfrac{c}{4L}, f_2 = 5\,\dfrac{c}{4L}$, etc.

The relationship between the natural frequencies is therefore

$f_1 = 3f_0, f_2 = 5f_0, f_3 = 7f_0$, and so on.

These frequencies are thus seen to be very simply related to each other; in fact if we had analysed the wave motion in a pipe open at both ends, we would have found an even simpler relationship, namely that the frequencies would have been related in the ratios of the natural numbers 1, 2, 3, 4, ...; that is,

$f_2 = 2f_1, f_3 = 3f_1$, and so on.

The reason why we did not analyse this case was that it did not give an opportunity to apply the two different kinds of boundary condition provided by the pipe closed at one end and open at the other.

We are now in a position to see why the pipe is such an important constituent part of some musical instruments. Taking the open–open pipe as our example, we have already seen that the normal mode frequencies are f_1, $2f_1$, $3f_1$, $4f_1$, etc. This is the *harmonic* series with f_1, the *first harmonic* (or *fundamental*), f_2 the *second harmonic* and so on. If the first eight of these could be successively sounded in ascending order of harmonics, and if the fundamental happened (for example) to be C below the bass stave, the musical effect would be as follows:

With the exception of the seventh harmonic, which is an excruciatingly flat B♭ (for which reason we have put the note in brackets) the first eight harmonics are all notes to be found on the western scale; in fact, the musical reader will immediately recognize them as forming the common chord of C major.

Since the general state of motion of the air in any pipe must be the sum of all the normal-mode solutions in varying strengths, depending on the method of exciting the motion, a given pipe can give out only frequencies in the harmonic sequence. These frequencies (for reasonably small harmonic number, at any rate) sound harmonious when heard in conjunction with each other. The musical nature of the sound from a pipe depends entirely on the fact that the natural frequencies for this acoustic system happen to be harmonically related to each other. The reason why a drum does not sound as musical as a pipe is that the natural frequencies of vibration of the drum head are related to each other in a very complicated way (in fact it may be shown that

$$f_2 \simeq 1{\cdot}5933 f_1, f_3 \simeq 2{\cdot}1355 f_1, f_4 \simeq 2{\cdot}2954 f_1, \text{ and so on})$$

and the effect of these when heard simultaneously is nowhere near as harmonious as that from a pipe.

A little more should be said about the boundary condition **8.5** for the open end of a pipe. Strictly speaking, the problem is much more complex than was apparent from our analysis. There is some acoustic pressure just outside the open end and our justification for assuming there was none was that the acoustic pressure outside was much less than that inside. More accurate (and complicated) analysis shows that the approximation is such that the pipe appears to be operating with an effective length slightly larger than its physical length. The extra length to make the frequencies observed fit the theory has been shown from experimentation and theoretical analysis to be about $0{\cdot}6R$ where R is the radius of the pipe. This is known as the *end-correction*. Further, the end-correction has been shown to depend very slightly on the wavelength, with the consequence that the harmonics are progressively more out of tune with an integral multiple of the fundamental as the harmonic number increases. But this is not, in most cases, a large enough deviation to worry the listener.

Another way in which the theory is approximate is that we have tacitly assumed that no acoustical energy is lost from the pipe, so that, once we have excited the air in the pipe, the vibrations will go on for an infinite time, even if we terminate the excitation. That this is not so is a matter of common observation; organ pipes, for example, cease to speak as soon as the organist takes his fingers (or feet) off the keys. The reason for this lack of *motus perpetuus* is that the pipe radiates acoustic energy from its open end, and also, in practice, through the walls.

A final word should perhaps be said about the open–closed pipe. These are found, as well as open–open pipes, in organs, and they produce a tone which is significantly different from that given by the open–open pipe, since only the odd harmonics are present. The clarinet's distinctive tone is connected with the fact that, to a close approximation, it behaves as a closed pipe.

3 Waves on strings

We have said a great deal about transverse waves on strings as easily visualized examples of wave motion; our reason for discussing them still further is that strings, as well as pipes, form the bases of many musical instruments such as the pianoforte, harp, members of the violin family and so forth. They are thus very relevant to a discussion of sound.

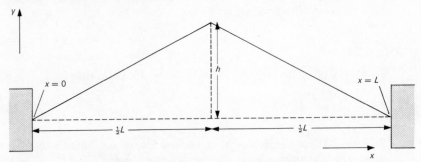

Figure 51 An example of initial conditions for a stretched string

Let us consider a string of mass per unit length μ, length L, under a tension T, fixed at both ends as shown in Figure 51. The wave equation **8.1** is valid for the stretched string, as we saw in Chapter 4, the velocity c, of transverse waves, in this case being $\sqrt{(T/\mu)}$. Our analysis will proceed much as that for waves in a pipe. First we need the boundary conditions; clearly, these are that the displacement y at each end of the string must be zero at all times. That is,

$$y(0,t) = 0 \qquad \qquad \textbf{8.12}$$
$$\text{and} \quad y(L,t) = 0. \qquad \qquad \textbf{8.13}$$

We take a typical normal-mode solution of **8.1** to be

$$y(x,t) = \phi_n(x)\cos(2\pi f_n t + \alpha_n) \qquad \qquad \textbf{8.14}$$

and, by an argument precisely the same as that in the last section we can obtain that $\phi_n(x)$ is the solution to the ordinary differential equation

$$\frac{d^2\phi_n(x)}{dx^2} = -\frac{4\pi^2 f_n^2}{c^2}\phi_n(x).$$

As before, therefore, the most general solution is

$$\phi_n(x) = a_n \sin\left(\frac{2\pi f_n}{c} x + \epsilon_n\right), \qquad \qquad \textbf{8.15}$$

and substitution of the boundary condition **8.12** yields the result $\epsilon_n = 0$. But the second boundary condition (**8.13**) differs from that in the previous section, and its implications can be seen by equating $\phi_n(L)$ in **8.15** to zero. This gives

$$a_n \sin \frac{2\pi f_n}{c} L = 0,$$

i.e. $\quad \dfrac{2\pi f_n}{c} L = 0, \pi, 2\pi, \ldots, n\pi, \ldots$

Thus the natural frequencies f_n are

$$f_n = \frac{nc}{2L}.$$

Since $c = \sqrt{(T/\mu)}$, the natural frequencies of the string are finally

$$f_n = \frac{n}{2L} \sqrt{\left(\frac{T}{\mu}\right)}. \qquad\qquad \textbf{8.16}$$

Equation **8.16** is an expression of *Mersenne's law*; we see immediately from it that the natural frequencies are a harmonic series, since

$$f_1 = \frac{1}{2L} \sqrt{\left(\frac{T}{\mu}\right)},$$

and therefore $\quad f_n = nf_1$.

The general motion of the string is a linear combination of all the normal modes, and therefore a string of given mass per unit length, under a given tension and of fixed length, can only give a combination of all its harmonics and no other frequency. This property, as we saw in the case of the pipe in the last section, is that which makes the string so suitable as the primary vibrator in a musical instrument.

Mersenne's law determines to a considerable extent the design, and in some cases the shape, of stringed musical instruments. By substituting $n = 1$ in **8.16**, which gives

$$f_1 = \frac{1}{2L} \sqrt{\left(\frac{T}{\mu}\right)}, \qquad\qquad \textbf{8.17}$$

we see that the fundamental frequency is determined exclusively by T, μ and L. Equation **8.17** determines, for example, the combination of the basic shape of the grand pianoforte, and the gradation in mass per unit length from string to string along the compass of the instrument. Suppose the lengths of all the strings in the pianoforte were the same, and further suppose all the strings were from one reel of wire. Then μ and L would be constants for the instrument, and the only way in which we could produce all the different notes over the instrument's seven-octave range would be by having the strings at different tensions.

Now, each octave rise in pitch means a doubling of the frequency; this means that the highest note on the instrument is of frequency 2^7 times that of the lowest note seven octaves lower. If the frequencies of the top and bottom note are denoted by f_t and f_b respectively, with corresponding string tensions T_t and T_b, then **8.17** tells us that, for constant L and μ,

$$\frac{f_t}{f_b} = \sqrt{\left(\frac{T_t}{T_b}\right)}.$$

Thus $\dfrac{T_t}{T_b} = \left(\dfrac{f_t}{f_b}\right)^2 = (2^7)^2 = 2^{14} = 16\,384.$

So, whatever other defects this arrangement may have, the frame of the instrument would have an absurdly uneven distribution of tension. Clearly, some other way has to be found to give us the seven octave range. In practice, all the possible variables, T, μ and L, are used to this end, but the gradations of μ and L are the most obvious. The strings are shorter for higher frequencies than for lower, giving the grand pianoforte its harp-like shape (the harp's shape is, of course, determined by the same reasoning). In addition the strings of the lower notes are thicker than those of the higher notes, having the effect of reducing the enormous length the instrument would otherwise have.

The increased mass per unit length for the lower strings is achieved in a rather interesting way. The strings are not simple thick strings; they are comparatively thin strings which are overspun – that is, a second wire is coiled tightly round the original wire over its whole length. The effect of this is to make the string flexible; a simple thick string would have somewhat rod-like characteristics so that transverse waves along it would, as was pointed out briefly in Chapter 1, be dispersive, causing the natural frequencies of the string not to be harmonically related to each other. In fact, even with overspun strings and simple strings for the higher notes, the natural frequencies are not harmonic because of stiffness (i.e. non-flexibility), but this defect is not sufficiently large to be noticed directly by the ear. Nevertheless it is a fact that a pianoforte, tuned so that the fundamental frequencies of all the notes are in tune, sounds badly out of tune, particularly at the higher end, and it may well be that the ear is taking as its criterion of pitch the upper harmonics of notes in the middle and lower ranges, rather than the fundamentals.

Mersenne's law (**8.16**) also determines some of the characteristics of instruments of the violin family. In these instruments, as in the case of the guitar and some other instruments, the different notes of the scale are obtained not by having a different string for each note, but by having a limited number of strings (only four in the case of the violin) whose effective lengths L are varied by 'stopping' the strings with the fingers of the left hand. The range of the instrument would be somewhat limited if only one string were used, and one of the purposes of the other three strings is to increase it. (Another reason for having more than one string is that several notes can be sounded simultaneously; this facility is extensively used in guitar music.) Furthermore, since the basic design is such that the four strings be of the same length, either the tension or the mass per unit length must be different for each string. Since it is undesirable that the tension be significantly different, causing the bridge of the instrument to be unevenly stressed, it is the mass per unit length that is different in practice. It is therefore necessary to buy a G-, D-, A- or E-string for the instrument, all of which are of different masses per unit length. The G-string is usually overspun with fine silver wire to increase μ, for the same reason as for the lower notes on the pianoforte. The D- and A-strings are usually made of gut (of different thicknesses) and the E-string, which has the highest fundamental, is usually made of fairly fine steel wire which combines the necessity for a small value of μ with that of mechanical strength.

We see, therefore, that Mersenne's law is basic to many aspects of the design of stringed instruments in that it determines the conditions which must be satisfied to obtain a desired fundamental frequency.

We will return to some other aspects of musical instruments later in this chapter, but let us for the present discuss some further properties of vibrating strings. We know that the general motion of a string must be some linear combination of its normal modes, and that, given the initial conditions, the strengths of the various harmonics can be determined. The typical normal-mode solution is (from **8.14** and **8.15**)

$$y_n(x,t) = a_n \sin\left(2\pi \frac{f_n}{c} x\right) \cos(2\pi f_n t + \alpha_n),$$

and since $\dfrac{f_n}{c} = \dfrac{n}{2L}$ and $f_n = nf_1$

from Mersenne's law (**8.16**),

$$y_n(x,t) = a_n \sin\frac{\pi n x}{L} \cos(2\pi n f_1 t + \alpha_n).$$

The general motion of the string is

$$y(x,t) = \sum_{n=1}^{\infty} a_n \sin\frac{\pi n x}{L} \cos(2\pi n f_1 t + \alpha_n) \qquad \textbf{8.18}$$

We can re-express **8.18** as

$$y(x,t) = \sum_{n=1}^{\infty} a_n \sin\frac{\pi n x}{L} (\cos 2\pi n f_1 t \cos \alpha_n - \sin 2\pi n f_1 t \sin \alpha_n).$$

We can replace $a_n \cos \alpha_n$ by C_n and $-a_n \sin \alpha_n$ by S_n, which gives

$$y(x,t) = \sum_{n=1}^{\infty} \sin\frac{\pi n x}{L} (C_n \cos 2\pi n f_1 t + S_n \sin 2\pi n f_1 t). \qquad \textbf{8.19}$$

The coefficients C_n and S_n depend on the initial conditions of the string, that is, on the positions and velocities of each point on the string at time $t = 0$. These vary, of course, according to the particular problem. For example, for a pianoforte string, the initial displacements $y(x,0)$ are zero, but the initial velocities depend on the shape, size and elastic properties of the hammer, and the velocity with which it hits the string. We will, however, not attempt to analyse this difficult problem; instead we shall take the problem of a string constrained into some shape described by the function $y(x,0)$, and then, at time $t = 0$, released. Our problem is to find the subsequent motion of the string with the aid of **8.19**.

The initial velocity of every point on the string is zero; our initial conditions can therefore be summarized by the fact that the initial shape is $y(x,0)$ and that

$$\left[\frac{\partial y}{\partial t} \right]_{t=0} = 0, \qquad\qquad 8.20$$

for all x.

Let us first find the effect of the initial condition **8.20** upon **8.19**. If we differentiate this latter equation partially with respect to time we obtain

$$\frac{\partial y}{\partial t} = \sum_{n=1}^{\infty} \sin \frac{\pi n x}{L} (-2\pi n f_1 C_n \sin 2\pi n f_1 t + 2\pi n f_1 S_n \cos 2\pi n f_1 t),$$

which, for time $t = 0$, becomes

$$\left[\frac{\partial y}{\partial t} \right]_{t=0} = \sum_{n=1}^{\infty} 2\pi n f_1 S_n \sin \frac{\pi n x}{L}.$$

Since this must be zero for all values of x, by **8.20**, it follows that all the coefficients S_n must be zero. So **8.19** assumes the simpler form

$$y(x,t) = \sum_{n=1}^{\infty} C_n \sin \frac{\pi n x}{L} \cos 2\pi n f_1 t. \qquad\qquad 8.21$$

To find the C_n we apply our knowledge of the initial shape $y(x,0)$ to **8.21**. At time $t = 0$, this equation becomes

$$y(x,0) = \sum_{n=1}^{\infty} C_n \sin \frac{\pi n x}{L}. \qquad\qquad 8.22$$

Suppose we wish to find a particular coefficient C_m; we merely multiply **8.22** by

$$\sin \frac{\pi m x}{L} dx$$

and integrate over the whole length of the string, obtaining

$$\int_0^L y(x,0)\sin \frac{\pi m x}{L} dx = \int_0^L \sin \frac{\pi m x}{L} \sum_{n=1}^{\infty} C_n \sin \frac{\pi n x}{L} dx.$$

Just as in our discussions on Fourier series, the nth term on the right-hand side is zero unless $n = m$, and the equation therefore reduces to

$$\int_0^L y(x,0) \sin \frac{\pi m x}{L} \, dx = C_m \int_0^L \sin^2 \frac{\pi m x}{L} \, dx.$$

The integral on the right-hand side of the latter equation can easily be shown to be $\frac{1}{2}L$, reducing the equation still further to

$$\int_0^L y(x,0) \sin \frac{\pi m x}{L} \, dx = \frac{1}{2} C_m L.$$

Finally, reverting to the nomenclature C_n rather than C_m, we have

$$C_n = \frac{2}{L} \int_0^L y(x,0) \sin \frac{\pi n x}{L} \, dx. \qquad\qquad \textbf{8.23}$$

So in the case of zero initial velocity, all we need do to calculate the C_n of **8.21** is to use our knowledge of the initial shape of the string, $y(x,0)$, together with the integral in **8.23**. It may seem surprising that Fourier series enter into this problem, and also that they arise in a spatial rather than a temporal way. This is so because the x part of the normal-mode solution contains the function $\sin \pi n x / L$ so central to Fourier theory; all we have then done is to multiply the equation by another suitable sine function which, upon integration, has yielded a zero result except for one term in the infinite series. The sine functions we have been using have the important mathematical property called *orthogonality*, which is that the integral of the product of any two of these functions over the appropriate limits is zero unless the two functions chosen are identical. It is this orthogonality property which is basic to analyses of this kind. If, for example, the string had not been of uniform mass per unit length, the normal-mode solutions would not have been sinusoidal in x and, in general, multiplication by a sine term and integration would not have solved our problem for us since there would be no orthogonality. However, sine functions are not the only orthogonal set, and functions orthogonal to the x-part of the normal-mode solutions can be used in the same way as the sine function in our analysis above.

To take a specific example of initial conditions, suppose the string is initially displaced in the manner illustrated in Figure 51. This profile, $y(x,0)$ has to be described by the two equations

$$y(x,0) = \begin{cases} \dfrac{2h}{L} x & 0 \leqslant x \leqslant \tfrac{1}{2}L, \\[2mm] 2h\left(1 - \dfrac{x}{L}\right) & \tfrac{1}{2}L \leqslant x \leqslant L. \end{cases} \qquad \textbf{8.24}$$

To find the motion of the string after the midpoint has been released (at time $t = 0$), we use **8.21**, in which the C_n are given by **8.23**. The integral on the right-hand side of the latter equation must be expressed as two integrals, one for the region between 0 and $\frac{1}{2}L$ (using the first function in equations **8.24**) and the other for the region between $\frac{1}{2}L$ and L (using the second function). From equation **8.23** we thus obtain

$$C_n = \frac{2}{L}\left[\int_0^{L/2} \frac{2h}{L} x \sin \frac{\pi n x}{L} \, dx + \int_{L/2}^L 2h\left(1 - \frac{x}{L}\right) \sin \frac{\pi n x}{L} \, dx\right],$$

which, after some rearrangement, becomes

$$\frac{LC_n}{4h} = \int_0^{L/2} \frac{x}{L} \sin \frac{\pi n x}{L} \, dx + \int_{L/2}^L \left(1 - \frac{x}{L}\right) \sin \frac{\pi n x}{L} \, dx.$$

Since x/L occurs frequently, we can simplify further by letting $x/L = z$, in which case $dx = L \, dz$. The last equation therefore becomes

$$\frac{C_n}{4h} = \int_0^{1/2} z \sin \pi n z \, dz + \int_{1/2}^1 (1 - z) \sin \pi n z \, dz. \qquad \textbf{8.25}$$

These two integrals may be evaluated by parts. Suppose u and v are both functions of x. Then, as is well known,

$$\int_a^b u \, dv = [uv]_a^b - \int_a^b v \, du. \qquad \textbf{8.26}$$

Applying **8.26** to the first integral, I_1 in **8.25**, with $u = z$ and $v = \cos \pi n z$, we obtain

$$I_1 = \frac{1}{\pi^2 n^2} \sin \tfrac{1}{2}\pi n - \frac{1}{2\pi n} \cos \tfrac{1}{2}\pi n.$$

By exactly similar reasoning we evaluate the second integral, I_2, in **8.25** as

$$I_2 = \frac{1}{2\pi n} \cos \tfrac{1}{2}\pi n + \frac{1}{\pi^2 n^2} \sin \tfrac{1}{2}\pi n - \frac{1}{\pi^2 n^2} \sin \pi n.$$

Thus $\quad I_1 + I_2 = \dfrac{2}{\pi^2 n^2} \sin \tfrac{1}{2}\pi n - \dfrac{1}{\pi^2 n^2} \sin \pi n$

$$= \frac{2}{\pi^2 n^2} \sin \tfrac{1}{2}\pi n,$$

since $\sin \pi n$ is zero for all n.

Equation **8.25** finally becomes

$$C_n = 4h(I_1 + I_2)$$

$$= \frac{8h}{\pi^2 n^2} \sin \tfrac{1}{2}\pi n.$$

Thus $\quad C_1 = \dfrac{8h}{\pi^2}, \qquad C_2 = 0,$

$$C_3 = -\frac{8h}{9\pi^2}, \quad C_4 = 0,$$

$$C_5 = \frac{8h}{25\pi^2}, \qquad C_6 = 0,$$

and so on.

The motion of the string with the initial conditions specified by **8.24** can now be obtained by substituting for the C_n in **8.21**, which gives

$$y(x,t) = \frac{8h}{\pi^2} \left(\sin \frac{\pi x}{L} \cos 2\pi f_1 t - \frac{1}{9} \sin \frac{3\pi x}{L} \cos 2\pi 3 f_1 t + \right.$$

$$\left. + \frac{1}{25} \sin \frac{5\pi x}{L} \cos 2\pi 5 f_1 t + \ldots \right), \qquad\qquad \textbf{8.27}$$

where the fundamental frequency f_1 is given by Mersenne's law as

$$f_1 = \frac{1}{2L} \sqrt{\left(\frac{T}{\mu} \right)}. \qquad\qquad [\textbf{8.17}]$$

Since the only frequencies present in **8.27** are harmonics of the fundamental frequency f_1, the motion of the string is periodic; that is to say, the profile of the string will assume, momentarily, its initial shape at the instants of time $1/f_1$, $2/f_1$, $3/f_1$ and so on. In practice this never happens, because the energy originally put into the string when it was drawn aside becomes dissipated due to the viscosity of the air, and to friction effects and non-rigidity at the supports. In the case of stringed musical instruments, it is the movement of the supports, driven by that of the string, which transmits the vibration to the belly or sound-board of the instrument which, in turn, vibrates to cause the sound waves in the air.

Finally, we did not take into account the fact that all strings, to a certain extent, have rod-like characteristics (i.e. they are not perfectly flexible); the frequencies of the normal modes are only approximately given by **8.16** and they are not quite harmonically related to each other. However, despite the lack of the inclusion of all these factors in our analysis (which would have made it extremely complicated), **8.27** does provide an understanding of the principles of the vibrations of a stretched string.

Formants

In the last section we analysed the transverse motion of an ideal stretched string and found that many of the properties of musical instruments could be accounted for. In this section we shall delve a little further into this topic and consider, in outline, the way in which the resonator (which may be the belly of a violin, or the soundboard of a pianoforte) modifies the vibrations originating at the string. Our reasons for persisting with this subject are manifold – musical sounds are in many respects the simplest kinds of all, and the physics of musical instruments, a subject worthy of study in its own right, employs principles which are applicable in many other branches of science.

The sound which we hear from a stringed musical instrument comes mainly from the cavity resonator to which the string is mechanically coupled, rather than from the string itself. This can be demonstrated quite simply by holding one end of a string of, say, one metre length and tying a weight to the lower end. When the string is plucked, very little sound emerges (although the string is under tension) because there is no suitable resonator attached to the string to cause enough of a disturbance in the air to produce an audible sound.

It is primarily the large vibrating surface area of the resonator which is responsible for the sound. Here we have a mechanical 'amplifier' which, in company with any other sort of amplifier, has different gains at different frequencies. For example, the gain of an audio amplifier (i.e. the ratio of the output voltage to the input voltage) varies with frequency, but a good amplifier will have a constant gain for most of the audio range.

Now let us consider the violin. The primary vibrators in the instrument are the strings, which generate a waveform whose spectrum (for a single note held for a long time) consists of delta functions at all the harmonics of the fundamental frequency. The various magnitudes of the delta functions are determined (within the limitations of our analysis in the last section) by the coefficients C_n in **8.21**. But these are not the 'strengths' of the harmonics of the note as we hear it, because, as we have seen, it is not the string which directly generates the sound wave, but the resonator activated by the string. The 'gain' of the resonator, because it varies with frequency, will modify the relative magnitudes of the delta functions, and the spectrum of the sound eventually emitted is this modified version. The resonator is said to exert a *formant* effect upon the 'signal' it receives from the string.

To illustrate further the meaning of the formant, let us suppose that, by some means or other, we have been able to excite vibrations in the string such that all the harmonics are of equal 'strength' – that is that all the delta functions in the spectrum of the signal provided by the string are of equal magnitude. The amplitude spectrum (we will not concern ourselves with the phases of these delta functions) is sketched in Figure 52. Now by exciting the resonator with a pure tone of variable frequency but constant amplitude, and observing, with a microphone connected to a voltmeter, the magnitude of the sound wave emitted into the air at different frequencies, we can plot a 'gain' versus frequency curve

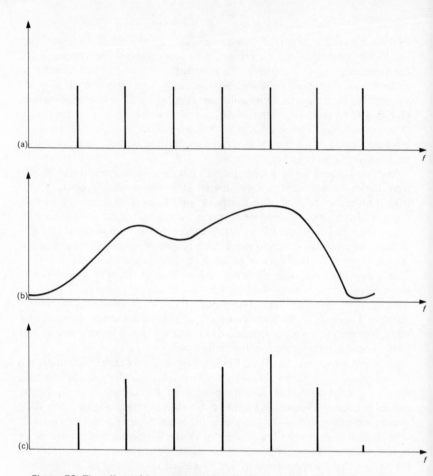

Figure 52 The effect of formants. (a) Amplitude spectrum of signal provided by vibrations of the string. (b) Amplitude formant characteristic of resonator. (c) Amplitude spectrum of sound wave emitted

for the resonator. (Again, we are not concerning ourselves with the phase of the output compared with that of the input, but just with the amplitudes.) This curve is called the *formant characteristic* of the particular resonator. An example of a formant characteristic is shown in Figure 52(b).

We are now in a position to determine the spectrum of the sound emitted. Since a pure tone of variable frequency produces output amplitudes as illustrated in Figure 52(b), then the signal illustrated in Figure 52(a) will, by the principle of superposition, produce an output whose spectrum is the product of the original spectrum and the formant characteristic. This is illustrated in Figure 52(c). Thus, in this example, although the fifth harmonic had originally the same amplitude as all the others, it will be amplified more than the others because the formant characteristic has its maximum at this frequency. So whatever the spectrum provided by the primary vibrator may be, the resonator will exert its formant effect upon it.

The extreme importance of the formant becomes very apparent when we consider the effect of playing different notes on the instrument. Suppose we continue our (admittedly rather unreal) hypothesis that the string is somehow being excited to provide a spectrum where the harmonics are of equal strength, and that we consider two different notes played by the instrument. The first note is that illustrated in Figure 52, which we have already dealt with. The second, which we will assume to be higher in fundamental frequency, is illustrated in

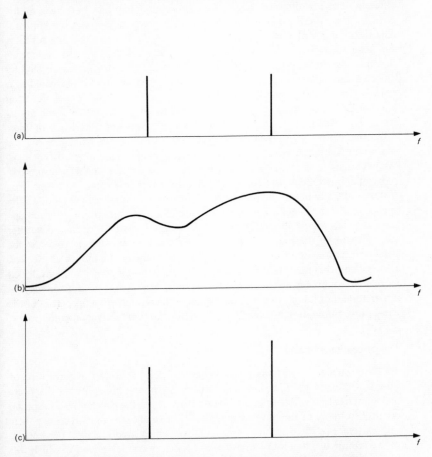

Figure 53 The effect of the formant of Figure 52(b) on a tone of higher fundamental frequency. (a) Amplitude spectrum of signal provided by the vibrations of the string. (b) Amplitude formant characteristic of resonator. (c) Amplitude spectrum of sound wave emitted

Figure 53. Here, in Figure 53(a), we see that the harmonics are further apart from each other than in Figure 52. The formant characteristic, however, is identical to that in Figure 52 because it is a property of the *violin*, and has nothing to do with the note being played. As a result of the variation in position of the spectral lines but constancy of the formant characteristic, we see that the fifth harmonic is no longer the strongest; it is the *second* harmonic now that is at a frequency corresponding to the peak in the formant curve, and it is this harmonic which is therefore strongest in the emitted sound.

It is thus the formant of the belly of a violin which impresses itself upon the harmonic content of whatever the performer is playing; although the spectra of different notes are different, they all have in common that they have been multiplied by the same formant characteristic. The frequency of the fundamental tells the brain of the listener what the pitch of the note is, and the formant characteristic, which 'colours' the spectrum of any note played, tells the listener that he is listening all the time to a violin. Indeed, since the formant is slightly different for different violins, enough 'formant information' is presented to a sensitive musically trained listener to enable him to distinguish one violin from another. It is interesting to speculate to what extent the 'Kreisler' tone differs from the 'Menuhin' tone by virtue of the formant characteristics of their respective violins as opposed to their different methods of playing.

Formants are clearly very important in musical and psychological acoustics. We have dealt so far with the 'fixed' formant – i.e. an unchangeable property of a particular instrument. But formants need not necessarily be of this type. For instance, the cavities in the human head provide a formant which modifies the spectrum of sounds made by the larynx. The characteristics of this formant can be changed at will by altering the shape of the mouth cavity. By doing so we alter the spectrum of the sound emitted when we speak or sing and in this case the listener interprets the formant for a particular shape of the mouth as a *vowel*. It is evident, therefore, that the auditory system contains a very well-developed formant-recognizing mechanism; exactly how this works is not yet clearly understood, but it is certain that this is one of the fundamental properties of the ear–brain combination in its capacity as an information receiver and interpreter.

8.5   **The perception of sound**

We have touched several times in this chapter upon the subject of perception of sound. Although the discussion has been mainly on the purely physical aspects of sound, it is impossible to isolate these entirely from the psychological aspects, because so many of the physical systems we have chosen to analyse owe their very existence to their use in musical contexts which involve sound perception. In this section we shall make a few general remarks about perception which will serve to augment what has already been said.

One of the most important facts about perception generally, and that of sound in particular, is summed up in the *Weber–Fechner Law*. We can best illustrate the ideas behind this law by a simple non-acoustical example. Suppose we blindfold a suitable volunteer, and put a gramme weight in his hand. Then if we add another gramme weight on top of the first he will immediately become aware that the total weight in his hand has increased. However, if we had started by putting a hundred-gramme weight in his hand and then added a further one-gramme weight the increase in weight would be so slight that he would be unable to notice it. So the pyschological effect of adding a given stimulus (namely the one-gramme weight) is profoundly affected by the magnitude of the stimulus which was already there.

The Weber–Fechner Law is a quantitative assertion which was originally based on research into the effects of placing additional weights on the hand. It states that the increase in stimulus necessary to produce a given increase in sensation is proportional to the pre-existing stimulus. In the context of our example it means that the increase in weight that would cause our volunteer to notice that it had been increased is proportional to the weight on his hand to start with.

To put this in more mathematical form, let us suppose that the original weight was W and that the just noticeable difference in stimulus, dS, is caused by the addition of a small weight dW. Then the assertion of the Weber–Fechner Law is that the dW which produces this must be proportional to W. If we let the constant of proportionality connecting these quantities be k, we have

$$dS = k \frac{dW}{W}.$$

Integrating both sides of this equation gives us

$$S = k \log_e W. \qquad\qquad \textbf{8.28}$$

Equation **8.28** is the mathematical description of the Weber–Fechner Law as usually stated.

Now how does this apply to the perception of sound? The first and easiest example is that of the pitch of a pure tone of given frequency. The *objective* quality in the tone is the *frequency f* which corresponds to the W in **8.28**; the *subjective* quality to be correlated with f is the *pitch* of the note, p, which corresponds to S in that equation. For pitch perception, therefore, **8.28** becomes

$$p = k \log f.$$

It is usual in this connection to define the constant k as $1200/\log 2$. Thus

$$p = \frac{1200}{\log 2} \log f.$$

The reason for this becomes apparent in the following way. An octave rise in pitch corresponds to a doubling of the frequency. Thus, corresponding to a frequency f_0 we have a pitch p_0 given by

$$p_0 = \frac{1200}{\log 2} \log f_0,$$

while the pitch p_1, corresponding to a note one octave higher than f_0, is

$$p_1 = \frac{1200}{\log 2} \log 2f_0.$$

Subtracting the two equations,

$$p_1 - p_0 = \frac{1200}{\log 2} \log \frac{2f_0}{f_0}$$

$$= 1200,$$

giving us the rise in pitch (on the scale we have defined) corresponding to one octave. Now on the equal-tempered scale, the octave is divided into twelve equal pitch increments of semitones (i.e. equal frequency ratios) namely from A to A♯, A♯ to B, B to C, and so on up to the A above; thus one semitone becomes equivalent to a pitch increase of $1200/12 = 100$ units. The original definition of the constant k as $1200/\log 2$ therefore produces the effect of dividing each semitone into a hundred parts; the unit of pitch resulting from this definition, which is widely used when discussing pitch, is called the *cent* (although other units have been devised for special purposes).

We see that the Weber–Fechner Law is particularly applicable when describing musical pitch. It is not in fact true for very high and very low frequencies in the audible range, but is a very good approximation over a range of several octaves.

Let us now consider the loudness of a pure tone. Just as pitch was the subjective correlate of frequency, so is loudness the subjective correlate of intensity. Experiments have been performed to find the just noticeable increase in loudness upon increase in intensity and it has been found that the Weber–Fechner Law holds reasonably well, the loudness L corresponding to the subjective quality S on the left-hand side of **8.28**, and intensity I to W on the right-hand side. The equation therefore becomes

$$L = k \log I. \tag{8.29}$$

Departures from the above relationship, however, occur at very high and very low intensities. We have already mentioned the case of low intensities; below a certain *threshold* of intensity no sound can be heard at all – it therefore follows that there can be no psychological correlate of *increase* of intensity below the threshold. The threshold is a function of frequency and is at its lowest for frequencies in the range 1–2 kHz (i.e. the ear is at its most sensitive in this frequency range). At high intensities the sensation becomes that of pain, and the relationship **8.29** breaks down.

It is usual to define a scale of L such that k is unity and the logarithms are taken to the base ten. Experiment has shown that the usual root mean square pressure threshold at a frequency of 1 kHz is about 2×10^{-5} Nm^{-2}. Let us designate the intensity corresponding to this pressure by I_0 and the loudness by L_0.

For an arbitrary intensity level

$$L = \log_{10} I,$$

while for the reference level I_0,

$$L_0 = \log_{10} I_0.$$

Subtraction of the second equation from the first gives

$$L - L_0 = \log_{10} \frac{I}{I_0}. \qquad \textbf{8.30}$$

On this scale of L, the difference in loudness is said to be $\log_{10}(I/I_0)$ bels, after A. G. Bell who did so much of the pioneer work in this field. This turns out to be a rather cumbersome unit as we quickly find out by means of a simple example. Suppose the intensity is initially I_1, with a corresponding loudness L_1, and is then doubled, giving a loudness L_2. Initially, therefore, **8.30** becomes

$$L_1 - L_0 = \log_{10} \frac{I_1}{I_0},$$

and after doubling I_1, it becomes

$$L_2 - L_0 = \log_{10} \frac{2I_1}{I_0}.$$

Subtraction of the first of these equations from the second yields

$$L_2 - L_1 = \log_{10} \frac{2I_1}{I_0} - \log_{10} \frac{I_1}{I_0}$$

$$= \log_{10} 2$$
$$\simeq 0 \cdot 3 \text{ bels}$$

– a rather small number for a twofold increase in intensity. In practice we therefore use a unit one tenth the size of the bel, called the *decibel*, abbreviated in most scientific literature to dB, and in most engineering literature to db. A doubling of intensity therefore produces an increase in loudness of $10 \times 0 \cdot 3 = 3$ dB.

As we have seen, 0 dB is defined as corresponding to a root mean square pressure p_0 of 2×10^{-5} Nm^{-2} at 1000 Hz. Since the intensity is proportional to the square of the acoustic pressure, **8.30** becomes

$$L - L_0 = \log_{10} \frac{p^2}{p_0^2} \text{ bels}$$

$$= 10 \log_{10} \frac{p^2}{p_0^2} \text{ dB}$$

$$= 20 \log_{10} \frac{p}{p_0} \text{ dB}.$$

The right-hand side of this equation defines the *sound pressure level* (abbreviated to SPL) corresponding to the root mean square acoustic pressure p. Thus

$$\text{SPL} = 20 \log_{10} \frac{p}{p_0} \text{ dB}.$$

Although the SPL is useful in psychological work in acoustics, it must be emphasized that it is itself not a subjective quantity at all, as the last equation shows. It is a function merely of the prevailing root mean square sound pressure and the standard p_0.

The SPL is used not only to designate the sound pressure of a pure tone in a form which has relevance to its perception, but can be extended to define the level of *any* sound whose root mean square pressure p can be determined. It is still, however, defined with reference to a pure tone of 1000 Hz and of root mean square pressure p_0 of 2×10^{-5} Nm^{-2}. To give some qualitative idea of the loudness corresponding to various SPLs the following list may be useful. An SPL of 15 dB corresponds roughly to the ambient noise inside a broadcasting studio, 60 dB to that in the average living room during a conversation, 100 dB to that inside an underground train, and 130 dB to the noise made by a pneumatic drill situated a few metres away. Beyond about 140 dB one feels a sensation of pain, and this value is the so-called *threshold of pain*.

Chapter 9
Light

9.1 The electromagnetic theory of light

9.1.1 *Introduction*

Although the wave nature of light had been established in the early part of the nineteenth century, when Thomas Young performed his classic interference experiment, it took a further half century before a satisfactory theory for light waves emerged. The great theoretical difficulty which had to be overcome was the explanation of how waves could be propagated in the absence of a medium, for all waves known at that time were mechanical in type and could not exist in the absence of a material medium.

The electromagnetic theory of light was formulated by James Clark Maxwell in 1860. Maxwell had developed a set of equations, now referred to universally as Maxwell's electromagnetic equations, which related electric and magnetic quantities, and, in fact, summarized all the then known properties of electric and magnetic fields. Maxwell showed that these equations could be processed in such a way as to yield a wave equation. He went on to show from this that electromagnetic waves could be propagated in free space, with a wave velocity which could be deduced from electrical measurements unconnected with wave phenomena, which turned out to be very closely the same as the velocity of light. The latter velocity had been approximately determined, over a hundred years earlier, by the astronomers Römer and Bradley, and later (more precisely) by Fizeau and Foucault.

9.1.2 *Electromagnetic waves in free space*

We will now follow in outline the arguments which led to the electromagnetic theory of light. We will start with Maxwell's electromagnetic equations for free space, which may be written as follows

$$\text{div} \, \mathbf{E} = 0, \tag{9.1}$$

$$\text{div} \, \mathbf{H} = 0, \tag{9.2}$$

$$\text{curl} \, \mathbf{E} = -\mu_0 \, \frac{\partial \mathbf{H}}{\partial t}, \tag{9.3}$$

$$\text{curl}\,\mathbf{H} = \epsilon_0\,\frac{\partial \mathbf{E}}{\partial t}. \qquad \textbf{9.4}$$

In these equations, the vector $\mathbf{E}$ is the electric field strength, the vector $\mathbf{H}$ is the magnetic field strength, ϵ_0 is a scalar constant known as the *permittivity* of free space, and μ_0 is also a scalar constant known as the *permeability* of free space. The operators div and curl are vector operators which enable the equations to be written in compact form. These operators are defined as follows. If $\mathbf{A}$ is a vector with Cartesian components A_x, A_y and A_z,

$$\text{div}\,\mathbf{A} = \frac{\partial A_x}{\partial x} + \frac{\partial A_y}{\partial y} + \frac{\partial A_z}{\partial z}; \qquad \textbf{9.5}$$

div $\mathbf{A}$ is a scalar quantity and is known as the divergence of the vector $\mathbf{A}$. If

$\mathbf{B} = \text{curl}\,\mathbf{A}$,

where $\mathbf{B}$ is a second vector with components B_x, B_y and B_z, then

$$\left.\begin{aligned}
B_x &= \frac{\partial A_z}{\partial y} - \frac{\partial A_y}{\partial z}, \\[2ex]
B_y &= \frac{\partial A_x}{\partial z} - \frac{\partial A_z}{\partial x}, \\[2ex]
B_z &= \frac{\partial A_y}{\partial x} - \frac{\partial A_x}{\partial y}.
\end{aligned}\right\} \qquad \textbf{9.6}$$

There is also a third vector operator which we shall refer to; this is gradient operator 'grad', which is defined in the following way. If $\mathbf{A} = \text{grad}\,\phi$, where $\mathbf{A}$ is a vector with components A_x, A_y and A_z, and ϕ is a scalar variable of position, then

$$\left.\begin{aligned}
A_x &= \frac{\partial \phi}{\partial x}, \\[2ex]
A_y &= \frac{\partial \phi}{\partial y}, \\[2ex]
A_z &= \frac{\partial \phi}{\partial z}.
\end{aligned}\right\} \qquad \textbf{9.7}$$

Equations **9.1**–**9.4** are expressed in SI units. These equations are deduced and fully discussed in *Basic Electricity* by W. M. Gibson (Penguin, 1969).

Now it can be shown by expressing a vector $\mathbf{A}$ in terms of its components and carrying out the operations described by **9.5**, **9.6** and **9.7**, that the following identity holds curl curl $\mathbf{A}$ = grad(div $\mathbf{A}$) $-\nabla^2 A$,

where ∇^2 is the operator

$$\left(\frac{\partial^2}{\partial x^2} + \frac{\partial^2}{\partial y^2} + \frac{\partial^2}{\partial z^2}\right).$$

If we operate upon both sides of **9.3** with curl we obtain

$$\text{curl curl } \mathbf{E} = \text{grad(div } \mathbf{E}) - \nabla^2 \mathbf{E} = \text{curl}\left(-\mu_0 \frac{\partial \mathbf{H}}{\partial t}\right).$$

But since div $\mathbf{E} = 0$ (from **9.1**) this becomes

$$-\nabla^2 \mathbf{E} = \text{curl}\left(-\mu_0 \frac{\partial \mathbf{H}}{\partial t}\right).$$

We can take curl within the differential coefficient with respect to t to obtain

$$-\nabla^2 \mathbf{E} = -\mu_0 \frac{\partial}{\partial t}(\text{curl } \mathbf{H}).$$

When we substitute for curl $\mathbf{H}$ from **9.4** we have

$$\nabla^2 \mathbf{E} = \mu_0 \epsilon_0 \frac{\partial}{\partial t}\left(\frac{\partial \mathbf{E}}{\partial t}\right) = \mu_0 \epsilon_0 \frac{\partial^2 \mathbf{E}}{\partial t^2}.$$

This final equation,

$$\nabla^2 \mathbf{E} = \mu_0 \epsilon_0 \frac{\partial^2 \mathbf{E}}{\partial t^2}, \qquad\qquad \textbf{9.8}$$

will be seen to have the form of the partial differential equation governing wave propagation in three dimensions. By comparison with the examples of Chapter 4, we note that the wave velocity $c = 1/\sqrt{(\mu_0 \epsilon_0)}$, and that the quantity which fluctuates (the disturbance) is the vector $\mathbf{E}$. The constant μ_0 is fixed arbitrarily by the definition of the ampere as unit of current; ϵ_0 is determined by experiment. It turns out that the values of μ_0 and ϵ_0 give c equal to the velocity of light in a vacuum.

If we repeat the same process, but taking the curl of **9.4** as the starting point, we arrive at

$$\nabla^2 \mathbf{H} = \mu_0 \epsilon_0 \frac{\partial^2 \mathbf{H}}{\partial t^2}. \qquad\qquad \textbf{9.9}$$

From **9.8** and **9.9** we see that both the electric field strength $\mathbf{E}$ and the magnetic field strength $\mathbf{H}$ vary in a wave manner in free space; variations of $\mathbf{E}$ and $\mathbf{H}$ exist simultaneously – we cannot have variations of $\mathbf{E}$ or $\mathbf{H}$ only. We shall now investigate what kinds of waves these are – whether they are longitudinal or transverse, or both.

Let us assume plane waves with direction of propagation parallel to the z-axis of coordinates. Let us also assume that there are no steady electric or magnetic fields. The wave fronts will therefore be parallel to the xy plane, and it follows from the definition of a wavefront that, at any given time, $\mathbf{E}$ and $\mathbf{H}$ must be constant over planes parallel to the xy plane, i.e.

$$\frac{\partial \mathbf{H}}{\partial x} = \frac{\partial \mathbf{H}}{\partial y} = \frac{\partial \mathbf{E}}{\partial x} = \frac{\partial \mathbf{E}}{\partial y} = 0. \qquad \textbf{9.10}$$

If $\mathbf{E}$ and $\mathbf{H}$ are resolved into their components E_x, E_y, E_z, and H_x, H_y, H_z along the coordinate axes, then, obviously, the derivatives of all the components of **9.10** will vanish also.

When we express **9.4** in component form, using the definition of curl given in **9.6**, we obtain

$$\left.\begin{aligned}
\frac{\partial H_z}{\partial y} - \frac{\partial H_y}{\partial z} &= \epsilon_0 \frac{\partial E_x}{\partial t}, \\[1em]
\frac{\partial H_x}{\partial z} - \frac{\partial H_z}{\partial x} &= \epsilon_0 \frac{\partial E_y}{\partial t}, \\[1em]
\frac{\partial H_y}{\partial x} - \frac{\partial H_x}{\partial y} &= \epsilon_0 \frac{\partial E_z}{\partial t}.
\end{aligned}\right\} \qquad \textbf{9.11}$$

On removing the terms which are zero from **9.10**, **9.11** reduces to

$$\left.\begin{aligned}
\frac{-\partial H_y}{\partial z} &= \epsilon_0 \frac{\partial E_x}{\partial t}, \\[1em]
\frac{\partial H_x}{\partial z} &= \epsilon_0 \frac{\partial E_y}{\partial t}, \\[1em]
0 &= \epsilon_0 \frac{\partial E_z}{\partial t}.
\end{aligned}\right\} \qquad \textbf{9.12}$$

A precisely similar analysis, but starting with **9.3**, yields

$$\left.\begin{aligned}
\frac{-\partial E_y}{\partial z} &= -\mu_0 \frac{\partial H_x}{\partial t}, \\[1em]
\frac{\partial E_x}{\partial z} &= -\mu_0 \frac{\partial H_y}{\partial t}, \\[1em]
0 &= -\mu_0 \frac{\partial H_z}{\partial t}.
\end{aligned}\right\} \qquad \textbf{9.13}$$

If we write **9.1** and **9.2** in terms of the components of $\mathbf{E}$ and $\mathbf{H}$, we obtain

$$\frac{\partial E_x}{\partial x} + \frac{\partial E_y}{\partial y} + \frac{\partial E_z}{\partial z} = 0,$$

and $\quad \dfrac{\partial H_x}{\partial x} + \dfrac{\partial H_y}{\partial y} + \dfrac{\partial H_z}{\partial z} = 0,$

which, on omitting terms which are zero from **9.10**, become

$$\frac{\partial E_z}{\partial z} = 0,$$

$$\frac{\partial H_z}{\partial z} = 0.$$

9.14

The last lines of **9.12** and **9.13**, together with **9.14**, given an extremely important result; they tell us that there is no variation of the z-components of either **H** or **E** with time or z-coordinate. In other words, plane electromagnetic waves have no longitudinal component. But from the first two lines of **9.12** and **9.13** we see that neither the time derivative nor the z-derivative of H_x and H_y vanish, from which we conclude that electromagnetic waves are transverse waves. Finally, we see from **9.12** and **9.13** that the x-component of **H** is related only to the y-component of **E**, and the y-component of **H** to the x-component of **E**. It follows from this that if **E** is entirely along the Ox axis (so that E_y and E_z vanish), then **H** must be entirely along the Oy axis. If we assume E_x has the form of a sinusoidal wave

$E_x = (E_x)_0 \sin 2\pi(ft - kz),$

then by **9.12** and **9.13**, and disregarding any steady fields, we find

$H_y = (H_y)_0 \sin 2\pi(ft - kz),$

where $(E_x)_0$ and $(H_y)_0$ are the respective amplitudes.

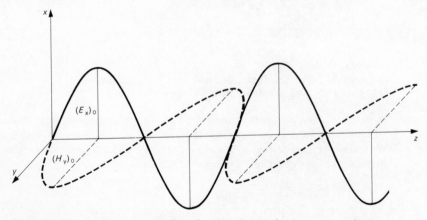

Figure 54 Perspective representation of a plane harmonic electromagnetic wave

We may represent them by means of a perspective sketch as shown in Figure 54. We note that the **E**- and **H**-components are exactly in phase with one another. It has been established experimentally that the electric vector **E** is responsible for light phenomena so that when we are discussing light waves, we may tacitly ignore **H**.

9.1.3 The electromagnetic spectrum

We have shown, starting from Maxwell's equations, that plane electromagnetic waves can be propagated in free space at the speed of light, and that the waves are transverse in character. Shortly after the appearance of Maxwell's theory of electromagnetic waves, Hertz provided experimental corroboration in which electromagnetic disturbances produced by an oscillating circuit were received by an isolated detector. Following the establishment of Maxwell's theory, a wide range of different types of radiation became recognized as electromagnetic waves of different frequencies (and therefore wavelengths). Radio waves, microwaves, infrared radiation, visible light, ultraviolet rays, X-rays and γ-rays are all examples of electromagnetic waves, differing from one another only in wavelength. They comprise the *electromagnetic spectrum*, which is illustrated in Figure 55. The wavelength range covered by the spectrum is

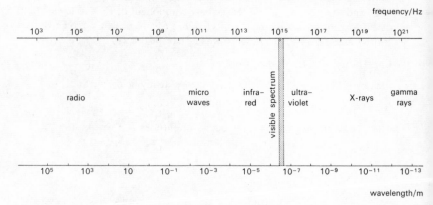

Figure 55 The electromagnetic spectrum.
(Frequency and wavelength plotted on a logarithmic scale)

enormous – from hundreds of miles for radio waves originating from distant nebulae down to one ten-thousand-millionth part of a millimetre for γ-rays. We see from Figure 55 that light waves – the only electromagnetic waves which stimulate the eye – cover only a tiny part of this spectrum.

9.1.4 *Electromagnetic waves in media*

So far we have only considered electromagnetic waves in free space. Maxwell's equations – as given in **9.1** to **9.4** – can be extended to cover a perfectly insulating, homogeneous, isotropic medium, containing no formal charges, merely by replacing ϵ_0 and μ_0 by $\epsilon\epsilon_0$ and $\mu\mu_0$, where ϵ and μ are numerical (dimensionless) constants, known respectively as the *relative permittivity* and the *relative permeability* of the medium. Such a medium is referred to as a *dielectric*; we are particularly interested here in dielectrics in which light waves may be propagated. If we repeat the analysis of section 9.1.2, but with ϵ_0 and μ_0 replaced, respectively, with $\epsilon\epsilon_0$ and $\mu\mu_0$, we arrive at the following partial differential equations in place of **9.8** and **9.9**:

$$\nabla^2 \mathbf{E} = \epsilon\epsilon_0\,\mu\mu_0\,\frac{\partial^2 \mathbf{E}}{\partial t^2}, \qquad\qquad \textbf{9.15}$$

$$\nabla^2 \mathbf{H} = \epsilon\epsilon_0\,\mu\mu_0\,\frac{\partial^2 \mathbf{H}}{\partial t^2}. \qquad\qquad \textbf{9.16}$$

We conclude from **9.15** and **9.16** that electromagnetic waves can be propagated in a dielectric with wave velocity

$$v = \frac{1}{\sqrt{(\epsilon\epsilon_0\,\mu\mu_0)}}. \qquad\qquad \textbf{9.17}$$

It turns out that ϵ and μ cannot be less than unity; in the case of a dielectric, μ is approximately unity but ϵ is greater than unity. Thus the velocities of electromagnetic waves in media are less than the velocity in free space.

If we reserve the symbol c for the wave velocity in free space, we see from **9.17** that

$$v = \frac{c}{\sqrt{(\epsilon\mu)}}. \qquad\qquad \textbf{9.18}$$

The *refractive index n* of a dielectric medium is defined as the ratio of the wave velocity in free space to that in the medium, i.e.

$$n = \frac{c}{v}; \qquad\qquad \textbf{9.19}$$

we see therefore from **9.18** that $n = \sqrt{(\epsilon\mu)}$. Since $\mu \simeq 1$,

$$n \simeq \sqrt{\epsilon}. \qquad\qquad \textbf{9.20}$$

Equation **9.20** would seem to indicate that the refractive index of a dielectric is constant. The quantity ϵ, however, turns out to be frequency dependent. If the value of ϵ measured by a statical method is used, then **9.20** holds reasonably well at low frequencies but breaks down completely at high frequencies.

9.2   Polarization

It was deduced in section 9.1.2 that plane light waves (indeed plane electro-magnetic waves in general) are transverse. The experimental evidence for the transverse nature of light waves is the fact that light waves can be *polarized*. Light beams obtained from most common sources (e.g. the hot gas in a discharge tube) are made up of a very large number of waves. The E-vectors of these waves (we are still assuming plane waves) are arranged in all directions in space normal to the propagation direction, and such light beams are said to be *unpolarized*. If the light is filtered in some way such that the E-vectors are suppressed in all directions save one, we are left with a unique direction of vibration and the light is said to be *plane polarized*.

Light may be rendered plane polarized in one of a number of ways. One method is by passing the light through a Nicol prism, that is, a pair of calcite crystals cut in a special way and cemented together. Another way is by passing light through a dichroic crystal – one for which the absorption of light is much greater for a given direction of vibration of E than for the direction perpendicular to it, so that if the light passes through a sufficient length of such a crystal, effectively all the amplitude in one direction is attenuated. This is the basis of the Polaroid method. A third method is by reflection; when a beam of light is directed on to a plane glass surface at an angle of incidence of about 57° (Brewster's angle), none of the light with electric vector vibrating parallel to the plane of reflection is reflected, so the reflected light is plane polarized, with vibration direction perpendicular to the reflection plane.

If a beam of light is plane polarized by, say, passing it through a Nicol prism, and then passed through a second Nicol prism which can be rotated about the direction of propagation of the light, it is found that for certain angular positions of the second prism no light emerges from it. This is incontrovertible experi-mental evidence that light waves are transverse. The first prism is referred to as the *polarizer* and the second as the *analyser*. If the polarizer and analyser are rotatable and are equipped with angular scales, this simple system can be used to investigate the state of linear polarization of any light beam. An application of this is in crystal physics, for many crystals polarize light, and analysis of the state of the light emerging from such crystals can yield important information.

9.3   Interference and diffraction

9.3.1   *Introduction – Huygens' principle and the scalar approximation*

These are subjects of very great importance and interest which really require a book to themselves. It is impossible here to do more than merely introduce them in a rather general way, and to show their significance within the wider subject of wave motion.

Interference takes place when light waves are superposed. Diffraction results when light waves are impeded or restricted in some way, for example, by placing an opaque obstacle in their path. It is enormously difficult to determine the effect of an obstacle on light waves from first principles. We should have first to find the electric and magnetic boundary conditions placed upon **9.8** and **9.9** by the presence of the obstacle, and then to solve the equations according to these

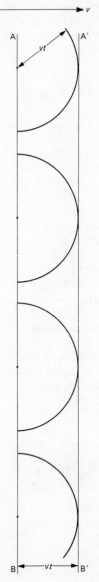

Figure 56
Rectilinear propagation of a plane wavefront

conditions. Fortunately, results, correct to a very good approximation, can be obtained in a very much simpler way by means of the *scalar approximation* and *Huygens' principle*.

According to the scalar approximation, the disturbance caused by a light wave may be represented by a single scalar variable when interference and diffraction effects are being considered (but not, obviously, for polarization). So with this approximation we can represent a plane harmonic light wave by

$$\phi = a \sin 2\pi(ft - kx),$$

where ϕ is the scalar disturbance.

Huygens' principle states that each point on a wavefront may be regarded as a new source of waves. It is relatively easy to show that Huygens' principle is consistent with the laws of rectilinear propagation, reflection and refraction. This we will now do, starting with rectilinear propagation. A plane wavefront AB (Figure 56) is moving in the direction of the arrow with velocity v; at any instant we may regard each point on AB as a source of secondary wavelets which give rise to spherical wavefronts. After a time t these wavefronts will all have radius vt and their common tangent A'B' will clearly occupy the same position as that the original wavefront will have reached after time t. Thus Huygens' principle is consistent with rectilinear propagation, as long as we choose to ignore the wave moving in the reverse direction which Huygens' principle predicts.

We will examine next the law of reflection. In Figure 57 a plane wavefront AB is shown incident at an angle of incidence i upon a plane reflecting surface XY at the instant when the point A has just reached the surface. We can regard A as a Huygens point source. In the further time it takes for B to reach the reflecting surface at D, the radius of the spherical wavefront emanating from A will grow to the value AC; since the incident and reflected waves are in the same medium, they will have the same velocity, so that AC and BD are equal. The reflected wavefront is obtained by drawing the tangent from D to the surface of the spherical wavefront at C, so that the normal to CD gives the direction of travel

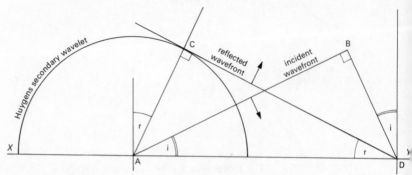

Figure 57 Reflection of a plane wavefront

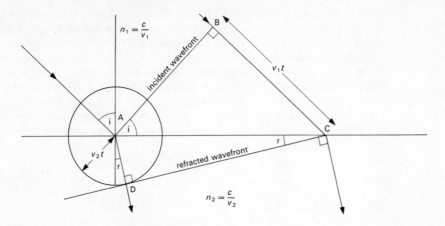

Figure 58 Refraction of a plane wavefront

of the reflected wave. We see at once that the triangles ACD and ABD are congruent; the angles BAD and CDA are therefore equal and the angle of incidence is equal to the angle of reflection.

A similar construction (Figure 58) leads to the law of refraction.

Here PQ represents the plane boundary between two media of refractive indices n_1 and n_2 respectively ($n_2 > n_1$). Again we have a plane wavefront AB incident at angle of incidence i on to the boundary and shown at the instant when the point A has just reached the boundary. Suppose the point B takes a further

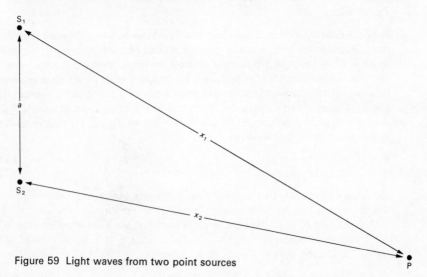

Figure 59 Light waves from two point sources

time t to reach the boundary at C, so that $BC = v_1 t$ (where v_1 is the velocity of light in the first medium). To find where the disturbance due to A has reached in this time, we regard A as a Huygens secondary source and draw a sphere of radius $v_2 t$ with centre A (v_2 is the velocity in the second medium). The wavefront in the second medium is represented by CD, the tangent from C to the section through the sphere in the plane of the drawing. The angle between the normal to CD and the normal to the boundary is the angle of refraction r. We note from the definition of refractive index **9.19** that, since $n_2 > n_1$, the velocity must be less in the second medium than the first. From the geometry of Figure 59 we see that

$$\sin i = \frac{BC}{AC} = \frac{v_1 t}{AC}$$

and

$$\sin r = \frac{AD}{AC} = \frac{v_2 t}{AC},$$

therefore

$$\frac{\sin i}{\sin r} = \frac{v_1 t}{v_2 t} = \frac{c/n_1}{c/n_2}, \qquad \text{from } \mathbf{9.19},$$

so that

$$\frac{\sin i}{\sin r} = \frac{n_2}{n_1}.$$

Thus the sines of the angles of refraction and incidence are in the same ratio as the refractive indices of the media on either side of the boundary and this ratio is constant for a given wavelength; this is the law of refraction or *Snell's law*.

9.3.2 *Interference*

We have established that Huygens' principle is reasonable by showing that the three fundamental laws of geometrical optics can be deduced from it; we now go on to apply the principle to try to account for the phenomena of interference and diffraction. Let us first investigate what happens when an observer receives light waves *simultaneously* from two point sources. Let the point sources S_1 and S_2 (Figure 59) be a distance a apart, and let the observer be at a point P at distances x_1 and x_2 from S_1 and S_2 respectively. Let us represent the disturbances at P due to the two light waves as

$$\phi_1 = a_1 \sin 2\pi(ft - kx_1), \qquad\qquad\qquad\qquad \mathbf{9.21}$$
$$\phi_2 = a_2 \sin 2\pi(ft - kx_2 - \epsilon). \qquad\qquad\qquad\qquad \mathbf{9.22}$$

Here, we are assuming that we have pure sine waves, both sources emitting with the same frequency and wavelength but different amplitudes. The epoch ϵ in **9.22** takes care of any difference in phase between the sources themselves. By the principle of superposition, the net disturbance ϕ at P is the sum of the individual disturbances ϕ_1 and ϕ_2. So we have

$$\phi = \phi_1 + \phi_2 = a_1 \sin 2\pi(ft - kx_1) + a_2 \sin 2\pi(ft - kx_2 - \epsilon). \qquad \mathbf{9.23}$$

For a fixed position P, the only quantity on the right-hand side which varies is t, so for convenience we will write

$$2\pi k x_1 = \alpha_1,$$
$$2\pi(k x_2 + \epsilon) = \alpha_2;$$

9.24

when we substitute these into **9.23** we get

$$\phi = a_1 \sin(2\pi ft - \alpha_1) + a_2 \sin(2\pi ft - \alpha_2).$$

When we expand the sine terms and factorize, this becomes

$$\phi = (a_1 \cos\alpha_1 + a_2 \cos\alpha_2) \sin 2\pi ft - (a_1 \sin\alpha_1 + a_2 \sin\alpha_2) \cos 2\pi ft.$$

If we now define two further quantities R and θ such that

$$R\cos\theta = a_1 \cos\alpha_1 + a_2 \cos\alpha_2,$$
$$R\sin\theta = a_1 \sin\alpha_1 + a_2 \sin\alpha_2,$$

and then substitute these into the previous equation, we obtain

$$\phi = R\sin(2\pi ft - \theta).$$

We see, therefore, that the net disturbance at P is simple harmonic in character, with the same frequency as that of the original waves, and of a phase angle relative to them defined by θ. It will be seen from squaring and adding $R\cos\theta$ and $R\sin\theta$ that

$$R^2 = a_1^2 + a_2^2 + 2a_1 a_2 \cos(\alpha_1 - \alpha_2)$$

9.25

and also that

$$\tan\theta = \frac{a_1 \sin\alpha_1 + a_2 \sin\alpha_2}{a_1 \cos\alpha_1 + a_2 \cos\alpha_2}.$$

It is worth noting, in passing, that **9.25** has the familiar appearance of the cosine formula for the solution of triangles. This suggests a useful graphical method for 'adding' two sine waves of the same frequency together. If we

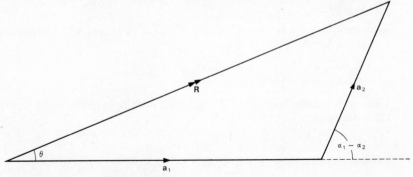

Figure 60 Vector addition of sine waves

represent the waves by two vectors whose lengths are proportional to the respective amplitudes of the waves, and the angle between the vectors is the difference between the phases of the waves, as shown in Figure 60, then the amplitude of the resultant is obtained (on the same scale) by completing the triangle, and the phase of the resultant with respect to the first wave is given by the angle between the respective vectors.

In the case of light waves, it is the intensity, not the amplitude, which is the important quantity. Detectors of light waves, such as the eye and photographic film, all respond to intensity. Indeed, there is no known method of measuring light amplitude directly. We saw at the end of Chapter 5 that intensity is proportional to the square of the amplitude, for waves in strings. This is also true for light waves, so we may take R^2 (**9.25**) as a measure of the way in which the intensity due to the superposition of our two light waves varies from place to place as we move P around. (Strictly, as P moves, a_1 and a_2 will vary, since we are dealing with spherical waves; we will, however, ignore this variation, and for a full treatment the reader is referred to N. Feather, *Vibrations and Waves*, Penguin, 1964, pp. 192–5.) For convenience we will put $a_1 = a_2 = a$, and assume that the two sources S_1 and S_2 are exactly in phase with each other, so that $\epsilon = 0$. When we make these simplifications, we find that **9.25** becomes

$$R^2 = 2a^2[1 + \cos(\alpha_1 - \alpha_2)].$$

Thus R^2 is maximum when

$$\cos(\alpha_1 - \alpha_2) = +1,$$
i.e. when $\quad \alpha_1 - \alpha_2 = 2n\pi;$ **9.26**

and minimum (zero) when

$$\cos(\alpha_1 - \alpha_2) = -1,$$
i.e. when $\quad \alpha_1 - \alpha_2 = (2n + 1)\pi.$ **9.27**

In **9.26** and **9.27**, n is zero or any positive or negative integer. But we see from **9.24** that

$$\alpha_1 - \alpha_2 = 2\pi k(x_1 - x_2),$$ **9.28**

since we have set ϵ to be zero. So the conditions **9.26** and **9.27** become, on replacing k by $1/\lambda$,

$$x_1 - x_2 = n\lambda \qquad \text{for maxima}$$
and $\quad x_1 - x_2 = (n + \tfrac{1}{2})\lambda \quad \text{for minima.}$

Thus, if P moves from place to place, we shall have maximum intensity ($R^2 = 4a^2$) when

$$S_1 P - S_2 P = n\lambda,$$

and minimum intensity ($R^2 = 0$) when

$$S_1 P - S_2 P = (n + \tfrac{1}{2})\lambda.$$

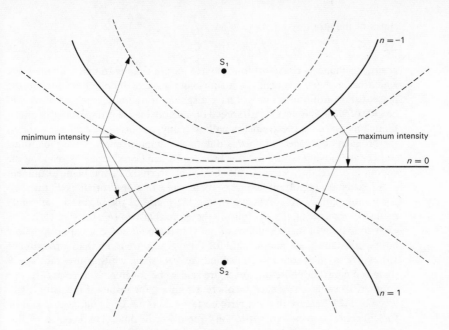

Figure 61 Hyperbolas of maximum and minimum intensity

If S_1, S_2 and P are always in the same plane, then the curves of maximum and minimum intensity form a family of hyperbolas, as shown in Figure 61.

One might suppose, on the basis of the above reasoning, that two point sources of light would produce a pattern of bright and dark lines of the kind shown in Figure 61. However, if completely separate sources are used, we do *not* get such a pattern. The reason for this is that – apart from lasers which are mentioned later – independent light sources do not fulfil one of the conditions that we have assumed, but without really saying so, namely that α_1 and α_2 do not vary with time.

To understand why we do not obtain such a pattern, we must pause for a moment to describe how light originates in common light sources. In a sodium-vapour lamp, for example, we have an assemblage of sodium atoms all moving about with random velocities. When collisions take place, the energy acquired in the collision process by one of the atoms may cause an electron in it to be excited into a higher energy state. Subsequently, the electron in the atom returns to its original state and in doing so releases a burst of light energy. This light energy is in the form of a light wave of very limited duration – of the order 10^{-8} s (i.e. a complete wave resulting from this process would take only 10^{-8} s to pass a point). It follows from the velocity of light in free space ($\sim 3 \times 10^8$ m s^{-1}) that the light waves would extend over about 3 m in space. The frequency f of such a light wave is related to the difference in energy ΔE between the two energy states of the atom by

$$\Delta E = hf,\qquad\qquad\qquad\qquad\qquad\qquad\qquad\text{9.29}$$

where h is Planck's constant. But we have seen in Chapter 6 that the only wave which has a single frequency is a sinusoidal wave of infinite duration, so the present short-duration wave will have a spread of frequencies whose mean will be the f of **9.28**. The wavelength spread of spectral lines resulting from this effect, though measurable, is extremely small. Actually, a considerable contribution to the broadening of spectral lines is due to the Doppler effect, since the atomic sources are moving randomly; this broadening can be reduced by streaming the vapour in a direction perpendicular to that in which the light is being examined.

An extremely important feature of these waves of atomic origin is that when a given atom emits two successive waves, the phase of the second is randomly related to that of the first. It follows therefore that two separate light sources, each consisting of many millions of individual atomic sources, cannot possibly have a constant phase relationship for times which are more than a fraction of 10^{-8} s. We say that sources of this kind are *incoherent*, whilst sources for which there is a constant phase difference are said to be coherent with respect to one another. If we have two such incoherent sources, the resultant intensity is still given by **9.25** – except that the term $\cos(\alpha_1 - \alpha_2)$ is not constant, as it would be for coherent sources, but varies very rapidly with time. The average of this quantity over a long time is zero, so the resultant will be

$$R^2 = a_1^2 + a_2^2.$$

That is, for incoherent sources, the resultant is everywhere just the sum of the individual intensities, and consequently there is no pattern of maximum and minimum intensity of the kind shown in Figure 61.

The simplest way to overcome this problem of incoherence is to derive both sources from a common original source. One way of doing this is shown in Figure 62, in which the light waves emanating from a point source S fall on to two pinholes S_1 and S_2 in an otherwise opaque screen. By Huygens' principle, S_1 and S_2 act as sources of secondary spherical wavelets. In the region to the right of the screen, where these secondary wavelets superpose, we have the necessary condition to observe intensity variation, for a constant phase relationship between S_1 and S_2 is maintained. The pattern of intensity we see is known as an interference pattern, and the process which produces this is known as optical interference. At any point in the region where the interference pattern is clearly seen, we deduce that a disturbance arrives via S_1 at the same instant as another disturbance arrived via S_2, but that these two disturbances started off from S at times which differed from one another by only a small amount compared with 10^{-8} s.

In practice, it is much more convenient to use slits rather than pinholes for S, S_1 and S_2 in Figure 62. This arrangement is known as Young's slits after Thomas Young who first performed the experiment in 1807. If monochromatic light emerging from S_1 and S_2 is viewed at a distance D from the screen, which is

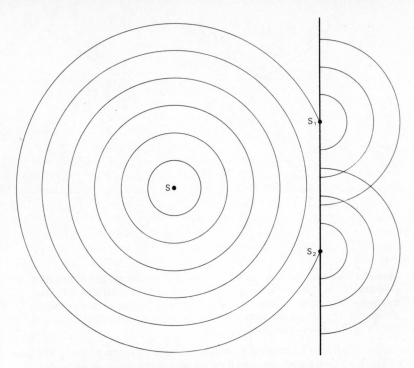

Figure 62 Coherent sources derived from a single common source S

very many times greater than the separation a of S_1 and S_2, then a series of alternate bright and dark fringes (Young's fringes) may be seen. It is relatively easy to show, though we will not do so here, that the fringes are equispaced and that the centres of adjacent bright fringes are a distance $\lambda D/a$ apart. Thus, if we wish to obtain distinct fringes of separation, say, half a millimetre with light of wavelength 5×10^{-7} m, we must arrange for the ratio of D/a to be 1000:1.

Young's fringes are an example of interference by *division of wavefront*, since the slits S_1 and S_2 select different portions of a wavefront in order to provide Huygens' secondary sources. Other common examples of interference by division of wavefront are Lloyd's mirror and Fresnel's biprism.

Another way of providing coherent sources is by making use of the fact that when light waves are incident upon a glass surface, part of the amplitude is transmitted through the glass and part is reflected. This is schematically shown in Figure 63. The physical situation at the interface is exactly analogous to that at the junction of strings of different densities discussed in Chapter 5. The two waves b and c emerging from the glass surface fulfil the conditions necessary for interference provided the time taken for c to traverse the extra path is small

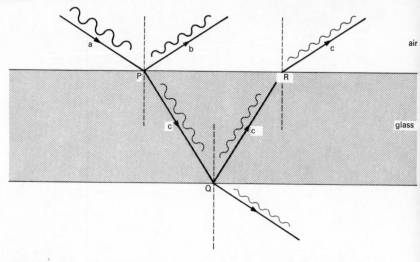

Figure 63 Coherent sources obtained by partial reflection of light waves at an air–glass interface. A light wave a is incident at point P. A part b of the wave is reflected, and a part c transmitted. After internal reflection at Q, c eventually emerges at R; c is coherent with b but will, in general, have a different phase since it has transversed an extra path

compared with 10^{-8} s. If these waves are brought into superposition, by means of a lens, we shall have brightness if the respective disturbances are in phase, but darkness if they are in antiphase. This is the basis of interference by *division of amplitude*, of which Newton's rings are the best-known example.

The above discussion applies to light waves derived from the sources which were available before the invention of the *laser* in 1960. The laser produces coherent light and consequently it is possible to obtain visible interference effects by superposing light from two separate lasers.

9.3.3 *Diffraction*

As we mentioned at the beginning of section 9.3, diffraction occurs when waves are limited or obstructed in some way. We shall consider the case of plane, monochromatic light waves incident normally upon a parallel-sided opening in an otherwise opaque screen. The experimental arrangement for this is shown in Figure 64. The plane wavefronts are derived from a lamp L with the aid of two converging lenses L_1 and L_2 and a restricting slit S_1. After passing through the diffracting slit in the screen S_2, the light waves are collected by a converging lens L_3. A screen arranged in the focal plane of L_3 will be seen to be illuminated by a series of bright and dark fringes; the central fringe which is situated on the optical axis of the system will be the brightest, with successive fringes above and below becoming rapidly fainter as we move away from the centre. This arrange-

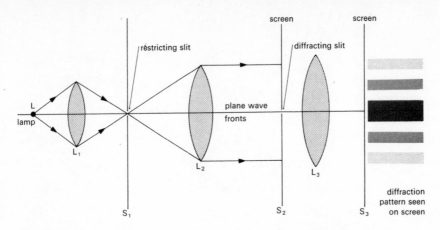

Figure 64 Experimental arrangement for obtaining single-slit diffraction pattern

ment of fringes is known as a diffraction pattern. It is entirely due to the restriction placed on the light waves by the slit in S_2, for if S_2 is removed, it will be seen that the diffraction pattern vanishes, being replaced by a single bright line which is the optical image of the illuminated slit S_1.

We will now see how this pattern can be accounted for. Figure 65(a) shows a given plane wavefront proceeding away from the slit of width a in the screen S_2. Suppose the direction of motion of this particular wavefront makes an angle θ with the optical axis of the system. The action of the lens L_3 is to collect together all the light along this wavefront and bring it to focus along a line on the screen S_3, indicated by P_θ in the section shown in Figure 65(b). The wavefronts for which θ is zero are focused at P_0 on the optical axis of the system. The total effect at the point P_θ is obtained by dividing the wavefront shown in Figure 65(a) into thin strips of equal width, the lengths of the strips being parallel to the length of the slit (i.e. perpendicular to the plane of the paper). Each strip will give rise to the same disturbance at P_θ, so we have to superpose the disturbances due to all the strips by the principle of superposition, taking account of any difference in phase between the individual disturbances. Now we note from equation **9.28** that

$$\text{phase difference} = \frac{2\pi}{\lambda} \text{ (path difference).}$$

It is apparent from Figure 65(a) that the difference between the paths travelled by the strips at the two extreme ends of the wavefront shown is just $a\sin\theta$. Thus the extreme phase difference ϕ is given by

$$\phi = \frac{2\pi}{\lambda} a \sin\theta. \qquad\qquad \textbf{9.30}$$

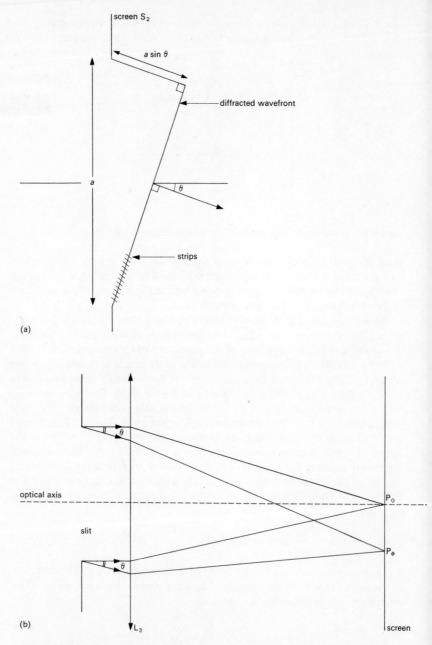

Figure 65 (a) Wavefront diffracted through angle θ. (b) Action of a lens in focusing wavefronts with different directions on to different positions on screen

Therefore the extreme phase difference across the wavefront is proportional to the distance apart of the strips concerned. It follows that the phase difference between disturbances due to any two strips is proportional to their distance apart, so that since the strips are all of equal width, the difference in phase between any two adjacent strips will have a constant value which we shall designate by δ. Let there be N strips and let the amplitude at P_θ due to each be b. We can find the net disturbance at P_θ by an extension of the vector method for superposing waves illustrated in Figure 60. Since we have a number N of disturbances to superpose, we have a polygon in place of a triangle, and the resultant is obtained by completing the polygon as shown in Figure 66(a). The vectors all

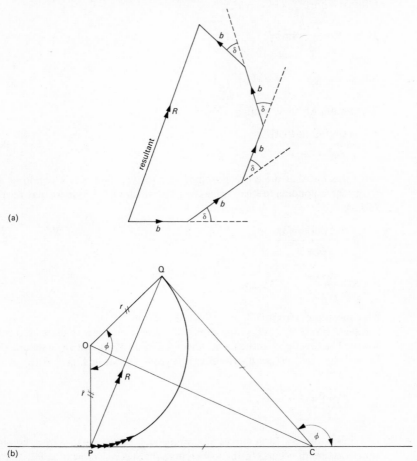

(a)

(b)

Figure 66 (a) Vector polygon for finding the resultant of a number of disturbances. (b) Vector diagram when individual disturbances become infinitely small

have the same length b, and each is inclined to its neighbour by the phase angle δ. We now let the strips become infinitely thin, and the number of them, N, infinitely large in such a way that the product Nb remains finite. As we go to this limit the vector polygon of Figure 66(a) becomes an arc of a circle, and the resultant R is the chord to this arc as shown in Figure 66(b). Let the arc have centre O and radius r. Clearly the extreme phase difference ϕ (see 9.30) is represented by the angle between the tangents to the two ends of the arc as shown.

We see from the geometry of Figure 66(b) that

$$R = PQ = 2r \sin \tfrac{1}{2}\phi$$

and that $\operatorname{arc} PQ = r\phi = Nb$.

Thus $R = \dfrac{2Nb}{\phi} \sin \tfrac{1}{2}\phi$.

But, since $\tfrac{1}{2}\phi = \dfrac{\pi}{\lambda} a \sin \theta$

(from **9.30**), we have, putting $Nb = A$,

$$R = \frac{A \sin[(\pi a \sin \theta)/\lambda]}{(\pi a \sin \theta)/\lambda} \, . \qquad\qquad \textbf{9.31}$$

It turns out that the diffraction pattern is only visible over a region of the screen corresponding to small values of θ, for which $\sin \theta \simeq \theta$, so we may rewrite **9.31** as

$$R = \frac{A \sin(\pi a \theta/\lambda)}{\pi a \theta/\lambda} \qquad\qquad \textbf{9.32}$$

or $R = \dfrac{A \sin \alpha}{\alpha}$ \qquad\qquad\qquad\quad **9.33**

if we substitute α for $\pi a \theta/\lambda$.

Equation **9.33** tells us how the amplitude varies from place to place across the screen. The function has the form shown in Figure 67(a), but since we are able to see only the *intensity* distribution, the curve shown in Figure 67(b) of the square of **9.33**, i.e.

$$R^2 = \frac{A^2 \sin^2 \alpha}{\alpha^2},$$

is of more interest. Both curves are symmetrical about $\alpha = 0$, where the zero-order maximum occurs. In the lower curve the successive maxima fall quickly away in agreement with the experimental fact mentioned earlier. In fact the zero,

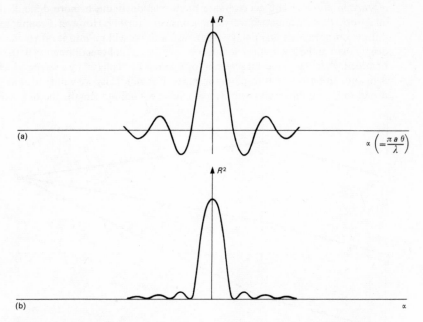

Figure 67 (a) Amplitude and (b) intensity distributions in single-slit diffraction pattern

first, second and third maxima in Figure 67(b) can be shown to be in the ratio $1 : \frac{1}{21} : \frac{1}{61} : \frac{1}{120}$.

It is also of interest to see the effect upon the pattern of altering the width of the diffracting slit. Now the nth maximum from the centre, at angular position θ_n, is defined by a particular value of α which we will call α_n. Since

$$\alpha = \frac{\pi a \theta}{\lambda}$$

by definition, then for the nth maximum, the value of $\pi a \theta_n / \lambda$ is constant. Thus $\theta_n \propto 1/a$, so that if we increase a, θ_n decreases, which means that the whole pattern closes in towards the centre. Similarly, if we decrease a, θ_n increases and the whole pattern expands outwards. This reciprocal relationship between size of slit and size of pattern is of considerable importance and interest in diffraction theory.

9.3.4 *Fraunhofer diffraction and the Fourier transform*

In the analysis of the last section the diffraction pattern was viewed at the back focal plane of a converging lens. Such a pattern is known as a *Fraunhofer diffraction pattern.* The general case of diffraction is much more difficult to analyse mathematically, and we will not consider it further. However, Fraunhofer diffraction presents some points of interest, and we will go into it rather more deeply than in the last section. Let us consider the Fraunhofer diffraction pattern obtained when the single-slit screen S_2 of Figure 64 is replaced by a screen which is opaque in parts and transparent in parts. For simplicity we will treat it as if it had only one dimension and was of effectively infinite length; the reader is

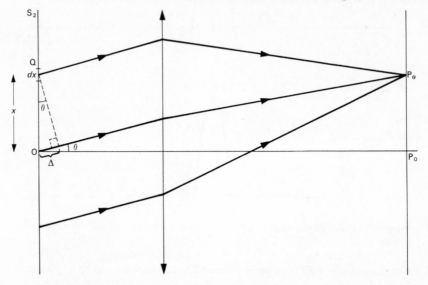

Figure 68 Normals to the wavefronts producing a Fraunhofer diffraction pattern on screen S_2

reassured that an analysis of a two-dimensional screen gives similar results (but only after rather greater algebraic manipulation). Let distance along the screen be x, as shown in Figure 68, and let the screen's transparency be $g(x)$. That is, those parts of the screen which are transparent have $g(x) = 1$, and those which are opaque have $g(x) = 0$. The screen S_2 is irradiated from the left by monochromatic light of wavelength λ. We consider plane wavefronts whose normals make an angle θ with the optical axis of the system. These wavefronts will eventually be collected by the converging lens L_3 (Figure 64) and focused at a point on the final screen S_3 corresponding to the angle θ. The amplitude of the net disturbance at this point will be the sum of the amplitudes (added together with due regard to phase) from each elemental length dx, such as the one shown at point Q. For the case $\theta = 0$, all the elemental disturbances, $g(x)\, dx$, from the whole screen S_2 travel the same optical path length to screen S_3 and therefore add up in phase to give the total disturbance at P_0 as

$$\int\limits_{-\infty}^{\infty} g(x)\, dx.$$

However, at non-zero angles θ we must account in our integral for the fact that all the elemental disturbances travel different optical distances in passing from the screen S_2 to P_θ, and therefore will no longer be in phase with each other. Taking the phase at the point O as zero, we immediately see from Figure 68 that the light being diffracted from Q at an angle θ and that diffracted from O through the same angle travel paths to P_θ which differ in length by Δ. This corresponds to a phase difference

$$\phi = 2\pi\Delta/\lambda.$$

Now from the geometry of Figure 68 we see that

$$\Delta = x \sin\theta.$$

Thus $\quad \phi = \dfrac{2\pi x \sin\theta}{\lambda},$

making the elemental amplitudes (in the complex exponential notation)

$$g(x)\exp(-i\phi)\, dx$$

or $\quad g(x)\exp\left[\dfrac{-2\pi i x \sin\theta}{\lambda}\right] dx$ **9.34**

instead of the rather simpler

$$g(x)\, dx$$

that we had for $\theta = 0$. In fact, we see that **9.34** reduces to $g(x)\, dx$ for $\theta = 0$, as indeed it should. So the disturbance at the point P_θ on the final screen is

$$\int\limits_{-\infty}^{\infty} g(x)\exp\left[-2\pi i x \,\frac{\sin\theta}{\lambda}\right] dx.$$

We now replace $\sin\theta/\lambda$ by S, so the disturbance, say $G(S)$ at P_θ is

$$G(S) = \int\limits_{-\infty}^{\infty} g(x)\exp(-2\pi i x S)\, dx. \qquad\qquad \textbf{9.35}$$

Examination of **9.35** shows that $g(x)$ and $G(S)$ are Fourier-transform pairs; we have thus demonstrated the remarkable fact (which more rigorous analysis confirms except for minor details) that the amplitude distribution in a Fraunhofer diffraction pattern is related to the transparency distribution in the original screen by Fourier transformation. Since the amplitude (or intensity) of the Fourier transform of any real function is even, it therefore follows that all

Fraunhofer diffraction patterns of partially opaque screens are symmetrical about the optical axis.

Let us now treat the example of the single slit of the last section by means of Fourier transforms. The screen S_2 is characterized by the function

$$g(x) = \begin{cases} 1 & |x| \leqslant a/2, \\ 0 & |x| > a/2, \end{cases}$$

where a is the width of the slit. Thus, by **9.35**,

$$G(S) = \int\limits_{-a/2}^{+a/2} \exp(-2\pi ixS)\, dx$$

$$= -\frac{1}{2\pi iS} [\exp(-2\pi ixS)]_{-a/2}^{+a/2}$$

$$= -\frac{1}{2\pi iS} [\exp(-2\pi i\tfrac{1}{2}aS) - \exp 2\pi i\tfrac{1}{2}aS]$$

$$= \frac{1}{\pi S} \left(\frac{\exp 2\pi i\tfrac{1}{2}aS - \exp(-2\pi i\tfrac{1}{2}aS)}{2i} \right)$$

$$= \frac{\sin \pi aS}{\pi S}$$

$$= \frac{a \sin \pi aS}{\pi aS}$$

$$= a \operatorname{sinc} aS,$$

a result identical in form to **9.32**.

We have in Fraunhofer diffraction, then, an important direct application of the Fourier transform. Diffraction patterns generally are related to the diffracting objects by an integral transform, but only in the case of Fraunhofer diffraction is the character of the transform normally simple enough to be interpreted with any ease. Fraunhofer diffraction is, moreover, very important in its own right. The diffraction of X-rays by crystals turns out to be of the Fraunhofer type; the amplitude distribution of the diffracted radiation is therefore related to the structure of the crystal (actually its electron density) by Fourier transformation, thus enabling us, in suitable circumstances, to deduce the atomic arrangement in the crystal from its X-ray diffraction pattern.

9.4   An instance of light not behaving as a wave

The wave theory of light, as developed from Maxwell's equations, has been completely successful in explaining all the observed optical phenomena relating

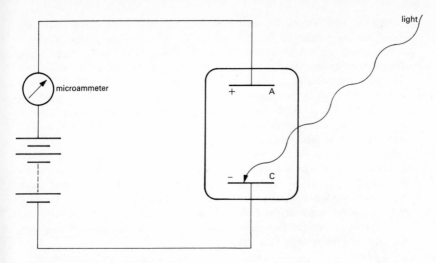

Figure 69 The photoelectric tube

to polarization, interference and diffraction. However, for some phenomena arising from the interaction of light with electrons in atoms the wave theory is quite inadequate.

An example is the photoelectric effect. When light is directed on to the surface of a freshly cut alkali metal, it is found that the surface becomes electrically charged. The effect may be demonstrated by a cell of the kind shown in Figure 69 in which a piece of alkali metal C is housed in an evacuated glass envelope. If electrode A is arranged at the opposite end of the tube, and C and A are connected in the circuit as shown, it is found that when the potential of A is made positive with respect to C, and visible light is directed on to C, a current flows in the circuit. A tube of this kind is known as a photoelectric tube and has many important applications, but our concern here is with the mechanism by which it works and, particularly, with the role of the incident light in this mechanism.

The polarity of A and C tells us at once that the current carriers within the tube are negatively charged and can therefore be immediately identified as electrons, since these are the only negatively charged entities in an alkali metal. If the light incident upon C is cut off, the current stops flowing, so we deduce that the light is somehow causing electrons to come out of the metal. Now it has been accepted for a very long time that metals contain electrons which are free to move about; this is why metals are good conductors of electricity. The electrons are kept within the confines of the boundary of the metal by means of a potential barrier at the surface, so that in order to escape from the metal an electron must acquire sufficient energy to surmount the barrier. In the above experiment, this energy must clearly be obtained from the incident light.

So far we have encountered nothing that cannot be explained in terms of the wave theory of light. But if we investigate the effect of varying the *frequency* of the incident light we are immediately confronted by a very strange result, for below a certain frequency, say f_0, it is found to be impossible to cause a current to flow in a given cell, no matter how intense the incident light is made. More sophisticated experiments show that, when the incident light is of sufficiently high frequency to cause a current to flow, the number of electrons emitted per unit time increases as the intensity of the light is increased (for fixed frequency) but that the velocity of the electrons escaping from near the surface remains constant. It is found that the *velocity* of these electrons can only be increased by increasing the frequency of the incident light.

None of this can be explained in terms of wave theory of light, for on this theory a given electron would eventually acquire sufficient energy to surmount the potential barrier no matter how low the frequency of the incident light. An explanation was offered by Einstein in 1905. Einstein suggested that instead of being spread uniformly over the wavefronts, the light energy is concentrated in packets or *quanta*, and that each *quantum* contains a fixed amount of energy E, related to the frequency of the light f by

$$E = hf,$$

where h is a universal constant (Planck's constant).

The quanta are to be regarded as discrete packets of energy which cannot be split up, so that if a light quantum strikes an electron within the metal, the electron acquires the whole of the energy hf of the quantum. If this extra amount of energy is sufficient to enable the electron to overcome the potential barrier, the electron escapes and contributes to the photoelectric current. On the other hand, if hf is less than that required to surmount the barrier, the electron remains within metal. Only in the extremely rare case of two quanta striking an electron simultaneously will the electron be able to obtain sufficient energy to escape.

We see that Einstein's theory explains why a more intense beam releases more electrons, but does not increase their velocity, for a more intense beam will have more quanta per second crossing unit area, but the energy of each quantum will be unaffected so long as the frequency does not change.

We see therefore that radiation has a dual character, acting in some circumstances as a wave phenomenon and in others as a particle phenomenon. However, it is not only light that is quantized in this way. Acoustical waves also behave in a quantum manner in certain circumstances. Electromagnetic quanta are known as *photons*, and acoustical quanta as *phonons*.

Chapter 10
Wave Mechanics

The Schrödinger equation

In the previous chapters we have discussed the principles of wave motion and have applied them to many different types of wave. The purpose of this final chapter is to discuss a more recent application of these principles, namely in the study of the properties of particles of atomic and subatomic size.

Up to the beginning of the twentieth century it was assumed that the principles of classical mechanics and electromagnetism could be applied to all problems in physics; indeed there was considerable justification for this assumption. Nevertheless, as the early years of the twentieth century passed, it became clear that classical physics was failing to account for an ever-increasing number of phenomena. We will not go into details here, as we are primarily interested in the wave-theory aspect of atomic physics rather than the subject itself; the reader who wishes to pursue the matter further is referred to the further reading list. We will, however, cite one experiment that would have produced puzzling results for the classical physicist. It was performed in 1927 by Davisson and Germer, and independently by G. P. Thomson, who directed a beam of electrons upon a thin foil of nickel. In Thomson's experiment, a piece of photographic film placed behind the nickel, when subsequently developed, showed a diffraction pattern, which was indisputable evidence of a wave phenomenon. Thus it appears that electrons behave both as particles and as waves. This is very similar indeed to the duality of light waves and photons discussed briefly at the end of Chapter 9. This dual nature of light had led de Broglie, prior to Davisson and Germer's experiment, to suggest that a corresponding duality might exist for electrons. Since particle dynamics had not proved satisfactory when applied to atomic systems, and since the wave nature of electrons had now been established, it became necessary to develop a completely new system of mechanics.

We will now develop, in outline, the *wave mechanics*, introduced by Schrödinger, in which the fundamental idea is that the dynamics of atomic particles are determined not by Newtonian physics, but by the properties of a wave function.

We start with de Broglie's hypothesis concerning the relationship between the particle properties and the wave properties of the particle. De Broglie postulated that the information about the momentum p of the particle was encoded in the wavelength, or more precisely the wave number k ($=1/\lambda$) of the wave. In fact he postulated that p was proportional to k, the constant of proportionality being Planck's constant. The postulate, expressed mathematically, is

$$p = hk. \tag{10.1}$$

We also use the result discussed at the end of Chapter 9 in relation to quanta that the total energy E of the particle is related to its wave frequency by

$$E = hf. \tag{10.2}$$

From **10.1** and **10.2** we shall infer the wave equation governing the wave associated with the particle. Suppose the potential energy of the particle is V. Taking (as we shall) a one-dimensional example for simplicity, we shall assume that the potential energy is a function, say $V(x)$, of the space coordinate x. The kinetic energy of the particle is $\frac{1}{2}mv^2$, where v is the particle's velocity. This can be re-expressed as

$$\frac{1}{2m} (mv)^2$$

and, since the momentum p is mv, the kinetic energy becomes $p^2/2m$. The total energy E is thus given by

$$E = \frac{p^2}{2m} + V(x). \tag{10.3}$$

If we substitute for E and p, from **10.1** and **10.2**, **10.3** becomes

$$hf = \frac{h^2k^2}{2m} + V(x). \tag{10.4}$$

From **10.4** we can infer the form of the wave equation. This latter will specify the wave-mechanical 'disturbance', known as the *wave function* of the associated wave. Let us call this function $\Psi(x, t)$. To obtain the wave equation from **10.4**, let us assume that it has a simple solution $\Psi = \exp 2\pi i(kx - ft)$. Then, differentiating this partially with respect to time once, and with respect to x twice, we obtain

$$\frac{\partial \Psi}{\partial t} = -2\pi i f \exp 2\pi i(kx - ft)$$

and

$$\frac{\partial^2 \Psi}{\partial x^2} = -4\pi^2 k^2 \exp 2\pi i(kx - ft),$$

which, by substituting the original Ψ for the exponentials, becomes

$$\frac{\partial \Psi'}{\partial t} = -2\pi i f \Psi'$$

$$\text{and} \quad \frac{\partial^2 \Psi'}{\partial x^2} = -4\pi^2 k^2 \Psi'. \qquad \textbf{10.5}$$

We see that equations **10.5** are linear in f and quadratic in k, as is **10.4**. Solving equations **10.5** for f and k, and substituting these into **10.4** gives

$$\frac{hi}{2\pi \Psi'} \frac{\partial \Psi'}{\partial t} = \frac{h^2 i}{4\pi^2 \Psi'} \frac{\partial^2 \Psi'}{\partial x^2} + V(x)$$

$$\text{or} \quad \frac{ih}{2\pi} \frac{\partial \Psi'}{\partial t} = -\frac{h^2}{8\pi^2 m} \frac{\partial^2 \Psi'}{\partial x^2} + V\Psi'. \qquad \textbf{10.6}$$

Equation **10.6** is known as the *Schrödinger equation* and is the wave equation governing the behaviour of atomic particles.

Physical interpretation of the Schrödinger equation

Introduction

In this section we will examine some of the implications of Schrödinger's equation. We must first discuss the significance of the wave function Ψ'. The first question we normally ask in a mechanical problem concerning a particle is 'where is it?' The answer to this question for an atomic particle is that, in general, we cannot determine precisely where it is – the most we can do is to determine the relative probabilities of its being at different points on the x-axis. Furthermore, these probabilities are related to the amplitude of the wave function, according to a hypothesis of Born (1926), by the equation

$$P(x,t)\,dx = \Psi'^*(x,t)\Psi'(x,t)\,dx. \qquad \textbf{10.7}$$

Here $P(x,t)\,dx$ is the probability of the particle, at time t, being between x and $x + dx$ and Ψ'^* is the complex conjugate of Ψ'. The right-hand side of **10.7** is, of course, real, as can be verified by multiplying any complex number by its conjugate; this results in the probability being, as it should be, a real number.

The reader may have sensed a paradox here. Since the Schrödinger equation (**10.6**) is linear, the solution Ψ' is indeterminate to the extent of a multiplicative constant. Any two solutions of the equation, when added together, form a further solution. It therefore follows, for example, that any solution Ψ', when added to itself to produce $2\Psi'$, will be a solution. How, then, can the probability of the particle being between x and $x + dx$ be related to the quantity $\Psi'^* \Psi'\,dx$ when this latter can assume any value we wish? The answer to this difficulty is that the information in $\Psi'^* \Psi'\,dx$ concerning the position of the particle is that of the *relative* probability of its being within a particular element of length dx

rather than another. To obtain the absolute probabilities, the wave function must be *normalized*. To do this, we note that, wherever the particle may be, it must be *somewhere* along the x-axis. Expressed in different terms, this means that the sum of *all* the elemental probabilities, defined by **10.7**, over all x must be unity since unit probability means certainty. So

$$\int_{-\infty}^{\infty} P(x,t)\,dx = 1$$

and therefore

$$\int_{-\infty}^{+\infty} \Psi^*(x,t)\Psi(x,t)\,dx = 1.$$

Thus, all we need do to normalize a solution to the Schrödinger equation is to multiply the function by its own complex conjugate and integrate over all x. This will result in some real number, say A. That is,

$$\int_{-\infty}^{\infty} \Psi^* \Psi \, dx = A,$$

with the consequence that

$$\int_{-\infty}^{\infty} \frac{\Psi^*}{\sqrt{A}} \frac{\Psi}{\sqrt{A}} \, dx = 1.$$

The normalization constant that we are seeking is therefore $1/\sqrt{A}$, because, when we multiply the given wave function by this quantity the resulting wave function multiplied by its own complex conjugate is a *direct* representation of the probability of the particle existing in a region dx around the value x.

10.2.2   *The particle in a 'box'*

Let us now consider a highly artificial wave-mechanical system, but one which gives a great deal of insight into the interpretation of the wave-function solutions to the Schrödinger equation. We consider the problem of an electron in a potential field such that the potential energy is zero in a certain limited region and infinity elsewhere. For simplicity we will assume, as before, that the problem is one-dimensional and that the range of zero potential energy extends from $x = 0$ to $x = L$, as shown in Figure 70. At these two values of x there are what are known as *potential barriers*, since an electron in the range of zero potential energy arriving at either $x = 0$ or $x = L$ would have to have an infinitely large kinetic energy to escape. The particle is thus confined within a 'box' of length L. Since the probability P of finding the particle outside the range is zero, it follows that Ψ also must be zero outside this range.

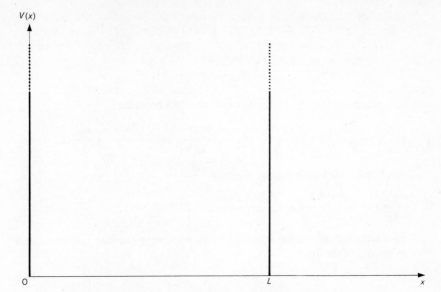

Figure 70 Representation of infinitely high one-dimensional potential well

The Schrödinger equation **10.6** for $0 \leqslant x \leqslant L$ is

$$i \, \frac{h}{2\pi} \, \frac{\partial \Psi'}{\partial t} = - \, \frac{h^2}{8\pi^2 m} \, \frac{\partial^2 \Psi'}{\partial x^2} \, , \qquad \qquad \textbf{10.8}$$

since $V = 0$. The general solution to this equation is the sum, with arbitrary coefficients, of all the normal-mode solutions. A typical normal-mode solution will be of the form

$$\Psi'_n(x, t) = \exp(-2\pi i f_n t)\psi_n(x),$$

where $\psi_n(x)$ is the x-part of the wave function corresponding to the nth normal mode of frequency f_n. Since the frequency multiplied by Planck's constant h is equal to the energy, say E_n (**10.2**), it follows that a unique energy is associated with a given normal mode. The expression $2\pi i f_n t$ is thus equal to

$$\frac{2\pi i E_n t}{h}$$

and the normal mode solution is therefore of the form

$$\Psi'_n(x, t) = \exp\left(-\frac{2\pi i E_n t}{h} \right) \Psi'_n(x).$$

Differentiating this last equation partially, once with respect to t, and twice with respect to x, we obtain

$$\frac{\partial \Psi_n'}{\partial t} = -\frac{2\pi i E_n}{h} \exp\left(-\frac{2\pi i E_n t}{h}\right) \Psi_n'(x)$$

and
$$\frac{\partial^2 \Psi_n'}{\partial x^2} = \exp\left(-\frac{2\pi i E_n t}{h}\right) \frac{d^2 \Psi_n'(x)}{dx^2}.$$

Substitution of these last two equations into **10.8** produces

$$i \frac{h}{2\pi}\left(\frac{-2\pi i E_n}{h}\right) \exp\left(\frac{-2\pi i E_n t}{h}\right) \psi_n(x) = \frac{-h^2}{8\pi^2 m} \exp\left(\frac{-2\pi i E_n t}{h}\right) \frac{d^2 \psi_n}{dx^2} x,$$

which, with some rearranging, becomes

$$\frac{d^2 \psi_n(x)}{dx^2} = -\frac{8\pi^2 m E_n}{h^2} \psi_n(x).$$

This ordinary differential equation is, by now, very familiar and its general solution is of the form

$$\psi_n(x) = A \cos 2\pi k_n x + B \sin 2\pi k_n x, \tag{10.9}$$

where $k_n = \pm \sqrt{\dfrac{2mE_n}{h^2}}$

10.10

To determine the coefficients A and B, we apply the boundary condition that $\psi_n(x)$ must be zero for $x = 0$ and $x = L$. Now, from **10.9**, $\psi_n(0) = A$, and since this must be zero it follows that $A = 0$. The solution **10.9** is thus simplified to

$$\psi_n(x) = B \sin 2\pi k_n x. \tag{10.11}$$

Let us now apply the boundary condition $\psi_n(L) = 0$. From **10.11**,

$$\psi_n(L) = B \sin 2\pi k_n L$$
$$= 0,$$

giving $2\pi k_n L = 0, \pm\pi, \pm 2\pi, \ldots n\pi,$
where n is any integer;

i.e. $k_n = \dfrac{n}{2L}.$

Substituting the value for k_n in **10.10** gives us

$$\frac{n^2}{4L^2} = \frac{2mE_n}{h^2}$$

or $E_n = \dfrac{h^2 n^2}{8L^2 m}.$

10.12

Thus, the energies corresponding to the various normal-mode solutions of Schrödinger's equation are in the ratio of the squares of the natural numbers. This brings us to another general point in the interpretation of wave-mechanical quantities, which illustrates the importance of the normal-mode solutions. Whenever a measurement of the energy of the electron is made, the electron is always found to have one or other of the discrete energy values defined by **10.12**. No other observed energies are permissible. We see, therefore the extreme importance of the normal-mode solutions and their frequencies. For this reason the normal-mode solutions to a wave-mechanical equation are called *eigenfunctions* (from the German *Eigenfunktion*, meaning characteristic function) and the values of E_n, or whatever other quantity is being investigated, corresponding to the normal frequencies are called *eigenvalues*. The number n is a *quantum number*. In this case, therefore, the energy eigenvalues are the only ones which are capable of being measured in this system. When we attempt to measure the energy of the electron we do not know which of the eigenvalues will eventually be measured, but *no value other than one of these* can possibly result. We have a similar situation in atoms, where electrons move in the potential field of the nucleus. This is why we have line spectra from atoms. Only certain definite wavelengths are contained in the emission spectra from atoms; these wavelengths correspond to certain definite frequencies, since $c = f\lambda$, which in turn correspond to definite energy changes.

0.2.3 *The velocity of a particle*

We now consider an interesting example of the relationship between a typical 'particle' parameter, namely velocity, and the wave-mechanical representation of this quantity. A given wave-mechanical problem may yield a wave function $\Psi(x, t)$ of the form of a set of travelling waves, where the velocity of each frequency component is slightly different from that of its neighbours in the spectrum, giving the effect of a 'group', as discussed in Chapter 7. From what has been said about the interpretation of $\Psi^*\Psi\, dx$ as the probability of finding the particle at a particular region in space, we may interpret the group velocity v_g as the velocity (in classical terms) of the particle. To show that this is so, we start from **10.1** and **10.2**

$$p = hk \qquad\qquad\qquad\qquad\qquad [10.1]$$
$$\text{and} \quad E = hf. \qquad\qquad\qquad\qquad [10.2]$$

The group velocity, as deduced in Chapter 7, is given by

$$v_g = \frac{df}{dk}. \qquad\qquad\qquad\qquad\qquad \textbf{10.13}$$

Now, from **10.1**,

$dp = h\,dk$

and similarly, from **10.2**,

$dE = h\,df$.

From these two equations we deduce that

$$\frac{df}{dk} = \frac{dE}{dp}.$$ **10.14**

But we have already seen that $E = p^2/2m$ (assuming zero potential energy); differentiation of this equation shows us that

$$\frac{dE}{dp} = \frac{2p}{2m} = \frac{mv}{m} = v.$$

The velocity v of the particle is therefore equal to df/dk (by **10.14**) which, by **10.13** is equal in turn to v_g. The group velocity of the waves is therefore identified with the classical velocity of the particle.

10.3   The Heisenberg uncertainty principle

We have seen all along that inherent in the structure of wave mechanics is the idea of probability. In general, the energy of a particle in a given situation is not a definite quantity causally determined, but is measured as one of a set of discrete energies. We saw also that the velocity of a particle is equal to the velocity of a group of waves describing the particle, so that the most we could say about the position of the particle was that it was most likely to be somewhere in the group.

This indeterminacy pervades the whole of the subject, and we see it as a consequence of the fact that we have to represent a particle by its associated wave function. Now, as we saw in Chapter 6, one of the properties of waves (and indeed of signals generally, whether they are propagated as waves or not) is summarized in the uncertainty principle, which was represented by the equation

$$\Delta t\,\Delta f \simeq \frac{1}{2\pi}.$$ [6.17]

What bearing does this wave property have upon the mechanics of subatomic particles? Equation **10.2**, namely $E = hf$, gives

$$\Delta E = h\,\Delta f$$

and therefore $\dfrac{\Delta E}{h} = \Delta f$.

Substitution for Δf in **6.17** gives

$$\Delta t\, \frac{\Delta E}{h} \simeq \frac{1}{2\pi},$$

which is $\Delta t\, \Delta E \simeq \dfrac{h}{2\pi}.$ **10.15**

Equation **10.15** is an expression of the *Heisenberg uncertainty principle*. It summarizes the fact that knowledge of when the particle is at a particular region and what the energy of the particle is cannot be precisely known simultaneously. For example, if a beam of electrons is stopped by a camera shutter, and the shutter is opened for a time Δt and then closed again, we know that a given particle has passed the shutter sometime during that interval Δt. If we then attempt to measure the energy of the emerging electron we will find that this latter quantity is indeterminate at least to the extent ΔE given by **10.15**. It is not a question of experimental technique, of sophistication of the apparatus used or the care with which the experiment was performed. It is inherent in the nature of the problem, and is a direct consequence of the fact that the dynamics of the particle are governed by the properties of waves, which themselves have this time-frequency indeterminacy.

Let us take two extreme examples. Firstly, suppose that the shutter in the experiment just described were opened for an effectively infinitely short length of time, so that ideally we know precisely when the particle was at a given place. If we call this time, for simplicity, $t = 0$, the time part of the wave function is a delta function at the origin, namely $\delta(t)$. The spectrum of this is, as we have seen, completely flat over all frequencies. We have, therefore, no knowledge whatsoever of the energy of the particle. The other extreme case is that in which the shutter is just left open for all time so that $\Delta t = \infty$. Here it is possible to have a perfectly monochromatic solution to the Schrödinger equation. The frequency is perfectly defined and therefore the energy, which is hf, is also perfectly defined and can, in principle, be measured as accurately as we like.

A similar situation obtains with the momentum and position of a particle. Just as a complex wave can be regarded as the sum of waves of different frequencies, so can it be regarded as the sum of waves of different wave numbers, and, since wavelength λ bears the same relationship to x as period τ does to t, we see that the k-spectrum of a wave can be obtained from the wave function by Fourier transformation from x-space to k-space. In fact, the wave uncertainty principle can be expressed in the form

$$\Delta x\, \Delta k \simeq \frac{1}{2\pi}$$

and, using **10.1**, we can obtain

$$\Delta x\, \Delta p \simeq \frac{h}{2\pi}.$$

This implies that we cannot simultaneously have precise knowledge of the position and the momentum of a particle and that, even using 'ideal' apparatus, the product of the uncertainties in the two quantities must be at least of the order of $h/2\pi$. In the case of the particle between the two potential barriers a distance L apart, $\Delta x \simeq L$ and the uncertainty in the momentum is of the order

$$\Delta p = \frac{h}{2\pi} \frac{1}{\Delta x} \simeq \frac{h}{2\pi L} \,.$$

Suggestions for Further Reading

General

H. J. J. BRADDICK, *Vibrations, Waves and Diffraction*, McGraw-Hill, 1965.

C. A. COULSON, *Waves*, Oliver & Boyd, 1952.

W. C. ELMORE and M. A. HEALD, *The Physics of Waves*, McGraw-Hill, 1969.

N. FEATHER, *Vibrations and Waves*, Penguin, 1964.

M. JAVID and E. BRENNER, *Analysis, Transmission and Filtering of Signals*, McGraw-Hill, 1963.

H. J. PAIN, *The Physics of Waves and Vibrations*, Wiley, 1968.

J. M. PEARSON, *Theory of Waves*, Allyn & Bacon, 1966.

D. H. TOWNE, *Wave Phenomena*, Addison Wesley, 1967.

Fourier series and Fourier transforms

R. BRACEWELL, *The Fourier Transform and its Applications*, McGraw-Hill, 1965.

H. P. HSU, *Fourier Analysis*, Iliffe, 1967.

R. C. JENNISON, *Fourier Transforms*, Pergamon, 1961.

C. A. TAYLOR and H. S. LIPSON, *Optical Transforms*, Bell, 1964.

Sound

A. H. BENADE, *Horns, Strings, and Harmony*, Heinemann, 1963.

W. A. VAN BERGEIJK, J. R. PIERCE and E. E. DAVID, *Waves and the Ear*, Heinemann, 1960.

L. E. KINSLER and A. R. FREY, *Fundamentals of Acoustics*, Wiley, 1962.

P. M. MORSE, *Vibration and Sound*, McGraw-Hill, 1948.

C. A. TAYLOR, *The Physics of Musical Sounds*, English Universities Press, 1965.

F. WINCKEL, *Music, Sound and Sensation*, Dover, 1967.

Light

J. W. GOODMAN, *Introduction to Fourier Optics*, McGraw-Hill, 1968.

S. G. LIPSON and H. LIPSON, *Optical Physics*, Cambridge University Press, 1969.

R. S. LONGHURST, *Geometrical and Physical Optics*, Longman, 1960.

H. D. YOUNG, *Fundamentals of Optics and Modern Physics*, McGraw-Hill, 1968.

Quantum mechanics

R. M. EISBERG, *Fundamentals of Modern Physics*, Wiley, 1961.

P. T. MATTHEWS, *Introduction to Quantum Mechanics*, McGraw-Hill, 1963.

L. PAULING and E. B. WILSON, *Introduction to Quantum Mechanics*, McGraw-Hill, 1965.

Problems

1   A U-tube having a uniform bore of area a with its limbs vertical contains a total length l of liquid. If the liquid in one limb is momentarily depressed through a small distance, oscillations ensue; determine the period T_0, neglecting friction.

    A bulb is now sealed on each end of this U-tube; when the liquid stands at the same level in each limb, the volumes of air enclosed above it are v_1 and v_2 respectively, and the pressure is equal to that exerted by a vertical column of the liquid of height h_0. The liquid level in one limb is again given a momentary depression. Assuming adiabatic conditions and neglecting friction, determine the period T of the ensuing oscillations of the liquid.

    Calculate the ratio of the specific heat of air at constant pressure to that at constant volume, given

$$T_0 = 0.63 \text{ s}, \qquad T = 0.54 \text{ s},$$
$$v_1 = 1.22 \text{ l}, \qquad v_2 = 1.20 \text{ l},$$
$$a = 400 \text{ mm}^2, \qquad h_0 = 780 \text{ mm}.$$

2   Two railway coaches of masses M and m are coupled together on a level, frictionless track by a light, elastic coupling of stiffness k. Originally at rest, they are set in motion by the coach of mass M being given an impulse from the end remote from the coupling. Find the period of the subsequent oscillations of the coaches. Find the numerical value of the frequency when $M = 1.5 \times 10^5$ kg, $m = 10^5$ kg and $k = 1.03 \times 10^6$ N m^{-1}.

3   A light spring of stiffness $2k$ is suspended vertically from a rigid support and carries a mass $2m$ at its free end. A second light spring of stiffness k is attached to the mass $2m$ and carries a mass m at its lower end. Deduce the natural frequencies and the normal modes of oscillation of the system.

    If the mass $2m$ is suddenly given a vertical velocity u when the system is at rest in its equilibrium configuration, derive the equation of motion for this mass.

4   A perfectly flexible elastic filament of negligible mass, stretched between two fixed supports at a distance l apart, carries three small masses, each of mass $\frac{1}{3}m$. One is attached at the centre and one at a distance of $\frac{1}{4}l$ from each support.

    Assuming the weight of the masses to be negligible in comparison with the tension F in the filament, calculate the frequencies of the corresponding principal modes of transverse vibration, and indicate their forms.

5   A plane sinusoidal sound wave of displacement amplitude $1 \cdot 2 \times 10^{-3}$ mm and frequency 680 Hz is propagated in an ideal gas of density $1 \cdot 29$ kg m^{-3} and at a pressure $101 \cdot 3$ kN m^{-2}. The ratio of the principal specific heats of the gas is $1 \cdot 41$. Find the pressure amplitude of the wave.

6   A small mass m is attached at a point on an indefinitely long string, of mass μ per unit length, in which the tension is F. A transverse wave of frequency f and of small amplitude travelling along the string is incident upon the mass. Derive expressions for the fractions of the incident energy which are transmitted and reflected at the mass, and find the phases of the transmitted and reflected waves relative to that of the incident wave.

7   A wire of cross-sectional area 10^{-6} m^2 is subjected to a tension of 10 N, and a harmonic wave with transverse and longitudinal components is propagated along its length. Calculate the frequencies for which the phase relationship between the transverse and longitudinal components is the same at two points on the wire separated by 1 m. (Assume that the waves are completely absorbed when they reach the end of the wire.)

Young's modulus for the material of the wire is 10^{11} N m^{-2}, and its density is 9×10^3 kg m^{-3}.

8   A periodic function $y(t)$, of period τ, is defined between the times $t = 0$ and $t = \tau$ as follows:

$$y(t) = A, \qquad 0 < t \leqslant \tau/4,$$
$$y(t) = -A, \qquad \tau/4 < t \leqslant 3\tau/4,$$
$$y(t) = A, \qquad 3\tau/4 < t \leqslant \tau.$$

Make a Fourier analysis of this function using the exponential form of Fourier's theorem, and display the results for the first ten harmonics graphically.

Make a Fourier analysis of the function $y(t - \tau/4)$ and display the first ten harmonics graphically.

Deduce the amplitudes of the first ten harmonics and comment upon the result.

Develop a method of Fourier analysing the function $y(t - t_0)$, where the analysis of $y(t)$ is already known (t_0 is a constant). Apply the method to Fourier analyse the function $y(t - \tau)$ and comment upon the result.

9   Show that the Fourier transform $X(f)$ of any real function $x(t)$ is Hermitian, i.e. that $X(f) = X^*(-f)$. Hence show that the amplitude spectrum of any real function is even.

10 If the Fourier transform of a function $f(x)$ is defined as $F(S)$, where

$$F(S) = \int\limits_{-\infty}^{+\infty} f(x) \exp(-2\pi i x S) \, dx,$$

prove the so-called shift theorem, namely that the Fourier transform of $f(x - a)$ is $F(S)\exp(-2\pi iaS)$.

Hence, or otherwise, find the Fourier transform of $f(x - a) + f(x + a)$. Use the result to explain qualitatively:

(a) what you would see in a Young's fringes experiment where the slits are of finite width;

(b) the general features of the spectrum of a sound heard with a single echo of itself;

(c) the general features of the spectrum of a pure tone of short duration.

11 A signal is sounded in a room so that an observer hears the original signal together with its echo a time T after the original, the signal and echo being of equal amplitude. Derive an expression for the spectrum of the composite signal in terms of that of the original one. At what frequencies is there zero amplitude in the spectrum? How would these frequencies be modified if the echo were the negative of the original signal?

12 A police car is equipped with a siren which emits alternately two notes, one of frequency 500 Hz, and the other of frequency 600 Hz. An observer standing near the road on which the car is moving observes that the pitch of the lower note as heard when the car is approaching coincides with that of the upper note as heard when the car is receding. If the velocity of sound in air is 745 m.p.h. and it is assumed that there is no wind, what is the speed of the car?

13 Deduce the expression for the pressure variations representing a pure tone of duration 5 seconds of peak acoustic pressure p whose pitch rises at a constant rate from an initial value of 200 Hz to a final value of 3200 Hz.

14 A uniform stretched string of linear density μ and length L under a tension T is initially displaced so that the points one quarter of the way from each end are oppositely displaced through a distance h leaving the centre point unmoved. The string is released from this position at time $t = 0$.

Assuming that $h \ll L$, deduce the nature of the subsequent motion of the string. What harmonics are missing?

15 Two pure tones, 0·1 Hz apart in frequency, sound simultaneously in an acoustically dead room. A sound-level meter placed in the room is observed to record 60 dB as its maximum reading and 20 dB as minimum. If zero dB is defined as corresponding to an r.m.s. acoustic pressure of 2×10^{-5} N m^{-2}, calculate the acoustic pressure amplitudes of each of the two pure tones.

Answers

1. $T_0 = 2\pi\sqrt{\dfrac{l}{2g}}, \quad T = 2\pi\left\{\dfrac{g}{l}\left[2 + ah_0\gamma\left(\dfrac{1}{v_1} + \dfrac{1}{v_2}\right)\right]\right\}, \quad \gamma = 1.41.$

2. $\dfrac{1}{2\pi}\sqrt{\dfrac{k(M+m)}{Mm}}, \quad 0.66$ Hz.

3. $\dfrac{1}{2\pi}\sqrt{\dfrac{k}{2m}}, \quad \dfrac{1}{2\pi}\sqrt{\dfrac{2k}{m}},$

   $x = \dfrac{2u}{3}\left(\sqrt{\dfrac{m}{2k}}\right)\sin\left[\left(\sqrt{\dfrac{2k}{m}}\right)t\right] + \dfrac{u}{3}\left(\sqrt{\dfrac{2m}{k}}\right)\sin\left[\left(\sqrt{\dfrac{k}{2m}}\right)t\right].$

4. $\dfrac{3}{2\pi}\sqrt{\dfrac{F}{lm}}, \quad \dfrac{3}{2\pi}\sqrt{\dfrac{3F}{lm}}, \quad \dfrac{3}{\pi}\sqrt{\dfrac{F}{lm}}.$

5. 2.20 N m^{-2}.

6. $\dfrac{k^2 F^2}{k^2 F^2 + \pi^2 m^2 f^4}, \quad \dfrac{\pi^2 m^2 f^4}{\pi^2 m^2 f^2 + k^2 F^4},$

   $\tan^{-1}\left[\dfrac{-\pi m f^2}{kF}\right], \quad \tan^{-1}\left[\dfrac{kf^2}{\pi m f}\right].$

7. $33.7n$ Hz, where $n = 1, 2, 3, \ldots$.

8.

0	1	2	3	4	5	6	7	8	9	10
0	$-\dfrac{2A}{\pi}$	0	$+\dfrac{2A}{3\pi}$	0	$-\dfrac{2A}{5\pi}$	0	$+\dfrac{2A}{7\pi}$	0	$-\dfrac{2A}{9\pi}$	0
0	$\dfrac{2A}{\pi i}$	0	$\dfrac{2A}{3\pi i}$	0	$\dfrac{2A}{5\pi i}$	0	$\dfrac{2A}{7\pi i}$	0	$\dfrac{2A}{9\pi i}$	0

11. Zero amplitude at frequencies $(n + \tfrac{1}{2})/T$, where $n = 0, 1, 2, \ldots$. If the echo is the negative of the original signal, zero amplitude occurs at frequencies n/T.

12. 67.8 m.p.h.

13. $p\sin(2\pi \times 360\exp 0.5545t)$.

14. $y(t) = \sum_n A_n \sin\dfrac{n\pi x}{L}\cos\dfrac{n\pi ct}{L},$

   where $A_n = \dfrac{16h}{n^2\pi^2}\left[\sin\dfrac{n\pi}{4} - \sin\dfrac{3n\pi}{4}\right].$

   The harmonic numbers of the missing harmonics are $1, 3, 4, 5, 7, 8, 9, \ldots$.

15. 1.43×10^{-2} N m^{-2}, $\quad 1.40 \times 10^{-2}$ N m^{-2}.

Acknowledgements

We are indebted to Miss Linda Cresswell, Miss Beryl Jones, Miss Beryl Rice and Mrs P. Tyrrell for assistance with the manuscripts; to Dr W. Gough for reading the draft; and to the University of Wales and University College of South Wales and Monmouthshire, Cardiff, for permission to reproduce examination questions.

Index

Acoustical energy 128
Aerial 117
Air, viscosity of 136
Amplitude 16, 96
  of a wave 38
Analysis, frequency 80
Angular frequency (or pulsatance) 17
Antinode 66, 127
Auditory system 121

Bandwidth 119
Barrier, potential 176, 182
Beats 31
Bel 143
Born, M. 175
Boundary conditions 68–72, 122, 124,
  127, 128, 129, 178
'Box', particle in a 176–9
Brewster's angle 152
Bridge (of stringed instrument) 132
de Broglie, L. 173
Bulk modulus 52

Carrier 117
  frequency 115
  wave 120
Cent 142
Charge oscillations 20
Clarinet 128
Classical mechanics 104, 173
Complex conjugate 96, 176
Constant, normalization 176
Constant, Planck's 174, 177
Curl (of a vector) 146
Current 89
Current and voltage waves in a line,
  velocity of 58–9
Cycle 15

D'Alembert's solution 60, 63, 69
Davisson, C. J. 173
Decibel 143, 144

Degrees of freedom 26
Delay line 59
Delta function 99–106, 117, 137
Demodulating 117
Dielectric 151
Differential equation, second-order
  linear 16
Diffraction 162–70
  pattern 163
Dispersion 12, 109–14
  anomalous 112
  normal 112
Disturbance 9
Div (divergence of a vector) 146
Division of amplitude 161, 162
Division of wave front (interference by)
  161
Doppler effect 107–9, 160
Double-sideband modulation 119
Drum 128
Duality, wave–particle 173

Ear 121
Eigenfunction 179
Eigenfunktion 179
Eigenvalue 179
Elastic string, waves in 49
Electric storm 121
Electromagnetism 173
Electromagnetic spectrum 150
Electromagnetic waves, in free space
  145–50
Electromotive force (e.m.f.) 89
Electron 173, 179
End-correction 128
Energy
  kinetic 174
  potential 174, 176, 180
  total 174, 177, 179, 181
  of travelling wave 75–8
Energy-density wave 77
Epoch 17

Equation, Schrödinger's 175, 177, 179, 181
Equation of simple harmonic motion 124
Ether, luminiferous 10
Exponential representation of a
  harmonic wave 40

Flex, wavelength of waves in 59
Formant 137, 140
Fourier, J. B. J. 79
Fourier
 integral 92
 mates 93
 series 104, 134
 transform 91–9, 101, 102, 103, 104,
  105, 117, 181
 transform, inverse 119
Fourier's theorem 79
Fraunhofer diffraction pattern 167
Frequency
 component 93
 fundamental 82, 87, 127, 130, 136, 137
 instantaneous 120
 natural 127, 130, 131
 of periodic motion 15
 spectrum 90, 98
Friction 136
Function
 'battlement' 85, 86, 87, 89
 characteristic 179
 delta 99–106, 117, 137
 even 95, 96
 non-periodic 91–9
 odd 96
 orthogonal 134
 periodic 79, 80, 82, 85, 86, 104

Gas, ideal 122
General solution of wave equation 60
Germer, L. H. 173
Grad (gradient of a scalar) 146
Greenwich time signal 93
Group velocity 109–14, 179, 180
Group, wave 111
Guitar 131

Harmonic 87, 127, 128, 136, 137
 waves 37, 38
Harp 129, 131
Heisenberg uncertainty principle 180–82
Hermitian 96
Hertz 150
Huygens' principle 154

Incoherent light sources 160
Information 92, 98, 119, 120, 140, 175
Initial conditions 61, 129, 133, 134, 136

Instruments, musical 127, 129, 132, 136
Intensity 142, 143
Interference 156–62
Invariance 90

Kinetic energy of string carrying a wave
  76
Kreisler, Fritz 140

Larynx 140
Light waves 91
Linear combination 123, 130, 132
Linearity 89
Lissajous' figures 22
Loudness 142–4

Maxwell, James Clerk 145
Maxwell's equations 145, 170
Mechanics, classical 104, 173
Medium 9, 121
 dispersive 110
Menuhin, Yehudi 140
Mersenne's law 130, 131, 132
Michelson and Morley experiment 10
Modulation 114
 amplitude 115–19
 frequency 120
 phase 120
Momentum 173, 181, 182
Motion, periodic 15

Natural frequencies, definition of 30
Newton, Sir Isaac 173
Nicol prism 152
Nodes 65
Normal modes 26, 123, 128, 129, 130,
  132, 134, 136, 177, 179
Normalized function 176

Octave 131, 142
Organ 128

Partial differential equation 37
Partial reflection 72–5
Particle 104
Particles, atomic 173–82
Percept 121
Period 15, 79
 of a wave 39
Permeability of free space 146
Permeability, relative 151
Permittivity of free space 146
Permittivity, relative 151
Phase 16
 angle 79
 change of, on reflection 73, 75

Phonons 172
Photoelectric tube 171
Photons 172
Pianoforte 129, 130, 131, 133
Pipes
 open–closed 122–8
 open–open 128
 organ 128
Pitch, musical 141, 142
Planck's constant 160
Polarization 152
Potential energy of string carrying a
 wave 75
Power in a wave 78
Pressure
 acoustic 123, 128, 143
 ambient 122
 waves in a gas 53
Probability 175, 176
Pulsatance 17

Quanta 172, 174

Radio communication 115
Radio waves 91
Rectilinear propagation 154
Red shift 109
Reflected wave 71
Refractive index 151
Resonance 115

Scalar approximation 154
Scale, equal-tempered 142
Schrödinger, E. 173
Sidebands 117
Simple harmonic motion 17
Sinc function 94, 95, 96, 97, 99
Sine wave 38
Single-sideband transmission 119
Snell's law 156
Sound
 infrasonic 121
 perception of 140–44
 pressure level 144
 ultrasonic 121
 waves 91
 waves, velocity of 55
Specific heats, ratio of principal 121
Spectrum 117
 amplitude 96
 band 95
 continuous 92
 line 98, 179
SPL 144
Standing (stationary) waves 64–7

Stiffness (of elastic string) 18, 131, 136
Straight-line wave 12
Strings, overspun 131
Superposition, principle of 69, 90, 110,
 138
Surface waves on a liquid 110
Synthesis 82

Temperature, ambient 122
Time-invariance 89
Thomson, G. P. 173
Threshold 121, 142
 of pain 144
Tone, pure 144
Transform pairs 93
Transmission line 13, 56–9
Transmitted wave 73
Trigger mechanism (of oscilloscope) 59

Uncertainty principle 98, 99, 180
Unmodulated cosine wave 120

Velocity of light in medium 151
Velocity of wave on string 51
Violin 129, 131, 137, 140
Vowel formant 140

Wave
 circularly polarized 12
 definitions of 10
 equation 121
 function 174, 175, 176, 179
 longitudinal 11, 121
 mechanics 173–82
 number 40, 174, 181
 profile 34
 transmitted 115
 transverse 10
 vector 46
 vector representation of 44–7
Wavefronts, spherical 48
Waveguides 13
Wavelength 39, 128, 174, 179, 181
Waves
 in fluids 51
 in a rod 55
 in strings 129–36
 in three dimensions 48
Weber–Fechner Law 140–42

X-ray diffraction 170

Young, Thomas 145, 160
Young's fringes 161
Young's slits 160